THE LIGHT OF GOD'S TRUTH AND MIRACLES:

The Awakening Has Started. My Burning Bush

45BUSTER

WESTBOW
PRESS®
A DIVISION OF THOMAS NELSON
& ZONDERVAN

WestBow Press books may be ordered through booksellers or by contacting:

WestBow Press
A Division of Thomas Nelson & Zondervan
1663 Liberty Drive
Bloomington, IN 47403
www.westbowpress.com
844-714-3454

Scripture taken from the King James Version of the Bible.

ISBN: 978-1-6642-4407-8 (sc)
ISBN: 978-1-6642-4406-1 (e)

Library of Congress Control Number: 2021918197

Print information available on the last page.

WestBow Press rev. date: 09/09/2021

PREFACE

To my children, family, and friends, this is my personal testimony I found in Jesus, my story of hope, life, and my greatest love, that I write.

I hope you read all of this and share with my grandchildren and their children and friends. I believe what God gave me is special—possibly the only documented miracles like this in modern times. And if I did not really believe that, I would not write it. God is my witness.

The Lord asked me to write this book back in 1997, but I was distracted by things of this world—mostly work.

INTRODUCTION

Welcome to my testimony of how God revealed Himself to me; you may find it hard to believe. I will share documented evidence for everyone to see, confirmed to me by His spirit in a personal relationship that took twenty-five years to build, moment by moment and day by day, and it's still ongoing. In the beginning when I experienced these thoughts and voices, I was not sure if it was God or just my thoughts. But after years of confirmation and different conversations with the Spirit of God, the documents God gave me proved that it was God, because no human has the ability to control time, space, and matter, as you will see.

As time went on, I started to discern between good and evil, the voice of God and my thoughts. Being attentive to the Spirit of God speaking to me led me to my salvation and also led me to having a closer relationship with Jesus. Eternal salvation, everlasting life in heaven, with Christ, is my greatest miracle.

Anyone can understand what I am going to say; I'll explain it in easy words, and the Holy Spirit will fill in the blanks for you.

On the day of Pentecost, Jesus sent the Holy Spirit, like a mighty wind (see Acts 2), breaking the barriers of language and giving the people understanding through His spirit because there were several tribes where people spoke different languages. In today's world, we still have His Holy Spirit giving us understanding, and of course, they write Bibles in all different languages so the language barrier is not a problem. There is a passage where Jesus calls the Holy Spirit, the Comforter. The Holy Spirit works in us to guide us and lift us up; to explain God's Word; and to give us discernment and comfort during times of trouble. Not only did He break the barriers of language, He gave the gift of the Holy Spirit on the day of Pentecost. Through the Spirit, God teaches us things humans do not have the ability to teach or show us.

Some readers may know a lot of the things I will be sharing. I hope first to help those who do not have much knowledge about the Bible or God. I was thirty-seven years old before I knew anything about the Bible. I promise, as you read about my experiences with God, you will understand why I say it is unbelievable. Trust me, even today, I think what God gave me is just out of this world; it's unthinkable. But then again, I know we serve a mysterious, out-of-this-world, loving God, full of grace and mercy and strength.

I love to read about experiences other people have had with God and how He finds His way into the life of His people. His methods are impossible for humans to replicate. God works in infinitely powerful ways, breaking all the human barriers like time, matter, and space to achieve His will. God does unbelievable things, and it is easy to know it was the Lord who did them. God did things in the past and showed people He can predestine our future. When you see God's hand at work or something has manifested for the good of your life, you should believe by faith God did it and be thankful. Hebrews 11:6 (KJV) says, "And without faith, it is impossible to please God: because anyone who comes to Him must believe that He exists and that He rewards those who earnestly seek Him."

Faith is believing without seeing. Jesus said, "Blessed be the man who has seen and believes, and bless the man who has not seen but still believes." I think He was talking about people who saw Him and believed and people, like us, who believe but have not seen Him. By faith, we should believe His Word in the Bible and what He does for us. We may not believe some things because we do not understand, but we should believe by faith, without seeing that God exists.

The Lord is actively working on our behalf, night and day, helping us have a better life now until the end, giving us knowledge and wisdom of Himself. That is exciting to me.

Some people say the Bible is full of contradictions and changes within different translations. This is true, not because the Bible is wrong, but because people interpret these words differently.

How can we know the Bible is the spoken Word of God and is accurate and true? By studying the Bible, you find it proves itself to be true. It is important to pray for understanding before reading the Bible. It's not like a newspaper you read once and throw away, it holds all things for all people in life, past, present, and future. The Bible is active, alive and living. It moves through time and changes according to circumstances and the will of God. No one has the ability to read and understand all of the Bible; it's a manual you need to study all your life. I believe God set it up that way for a reason; for example, you could read a passage today and understand it in one way, then read the same passage a year later and have a new understanding. When that happens, you see a new important revelation He has for you for the times you are in. This is why people say His Word is alive, moving to our everyday needs, changing through time. What book or newspaper offers that kind of knowledge? This is more proof it is from the Lord God.

Miracles still happen in the world today. My aim is to open up more people to the belief that your miracles are waiting to be discovered and received by faith. This book will help those who do not know Who God is, or do not understand His Word, or do not even believe there is a God. I did not understand the Bible for years; I was lost: a sinner, blind, hungry, thirsty, and dying without knowing Jesus in a personal way.

Keep in mind, my testimony is not fast food or instant breakfast. It is important to see that God has an overall plan for the redemption of humanity. The Bible is not just a bunch of stories; these tales come together in a wonderful, beautiful picture of life, love, mercy, grace, understanding, and eternal life. Yes, there is war, death, evil, bad angels, and good angels; they're all part of His plan. Understanding this helps us in many ways; finding our purpose in the big picture can give us some peace.

"Lord, you know who they are; please give them understanding, and let the light of Your truths open up the places that need it. Soften up what needs softening, and fill the reader with what they need, right now. In the name of Jesus, I pray. Amen."

About two thousand years ago, without human hands, God built His new covenant church in the truth, light, and the blood of Jesus. In Hebrews 9:1-11 (NIV) the old Jewish covenant built with hands passed away. In 2 Corinthians 5:17 (NIV), Therefore, if anyone is in Christ, the new creation has come. The old has gone, the new is here!"

The people who believed in Jesus had to hide in the shadows from the holy men, God's first covenant church, the Jewish people of their day. The Old Testament in the Bible is about how God started to set up His plan of salvation. The New Testament is about the virgin birth of Jesus and His life, death, and resurrection, the finished work on the cross. This is the completed plan of salvation for all the world that would believe in Him and call on His name. God had a requirement that the sin debt be paid with blood, and the blood had to be perfect in every way. The blood had to be from the Lamb of God, Jesus, His Son. The blood of Jesus paid the sin debt in full, past, present, and future. The blessing and Spirit of God are with the believers of Jesus in the new church. God is still working with the Jewish people. He has not given up on them and blesses who He wants. Few Jewish people back then understood that killing Jesus was part of the prophecies from the Old Testament; even after Jesus told His disciples He was going to die soon, they did not understand why. Not all of God's mysteries are revealed in one moment of time to all people. Isaiah and other prophets wrote in the Old Testament that they would kill their Messiah, their King. So again, the Word of God proves this is the plan He had. Some prophecies were written thousands of years ahead, and some were written hundreds of years before they happened. Jesus fulfilled over three hundred prophecies in His virgin birth, life, miracles, death, and resurrection.

The good thing in all this is more and more Jewish people are finding out this truth and coming to the knowledge of Jesus for their salvation, just like God's Word says would happen in the end days. You see how it is all coming together like the Lord said it would? Two thousand years ago, Christians had to be careful who they spoke to because they would be put to death if caught preaching the Gospel of Jesus, the Good News. The Jewish priests, holy men, and people of the day did not want to hear the truth about Jesus, especially if it meant changing something in their lives. They were comfortable. Some had power or money in high places, location, or religion, and they did not want to give up anything. Some sinners did not want to come to the knowledge of Jesus because they did not want to give up their sin. Even in today's world, if something gets in the way of people or threatens them, they kill it or make it go away somehow.

We can see the same thing going on in churches and in the culture of today's world: lies and fake, feel-good religions, and laws that say it's okay to kill things. It is our free will, and hopefully, after you read this book, you will choose the truth and respect God's Word and His creation. God's promises will come to pass. Read 2 Peter 3:10-12 (NIV): "But the day of the Lord will come like a thief, the Heavens will disappear with a roar, the elements will be destroyed by fire and the earth and everything in it will be laid bare. Since everything will be destroyed in this way, what kind of people ought you to be? You ought to live holy and godly lives. As you look forward to the day of God and speed its coming. Stand strong to the end and believe God keeps His promises." I like to read the whole chapter to get a better understanding of what the writer is speaking about.

The true church of God will be pushed back to the shadows of the streets and into the homes, out of the sight of the ungodly haters, the evil spirits, and the children of darkness. They do not want to see or hear the truth from God's Word or His peacemakers, the ministers of the Gospel. In today's world, the ungodly politicians make laws to stop the truth from getting out, starting with the Bible. In 2 Timothy 3:5 (NIV), the scripture says people will have "a form of godliness but [deny] its power. Have nothing to do with them."

The darkness took the Word of God out of the schools, out of public places, and soon it will be completely out of government. Soon after, our freedoms will be lost, one law at a time, creeping into every part of our life like a thief, deceived by the dragon, the devil Satan. Revelation 12:9 (NIV) says, "The great dragon was hurled down, the ancient serpent called the Devil or Satan who leads the whole world astray. He was hurled to the earth and his angels with him." Revelation 12:11 (NIV) says "They triumphed over him by the blood of the Lamb and by the word of their testimony, they did not love their lives so much as to shrink from death." So believe in God's plan, believe in Christ Jesus and live free.

The Bible says the world will not turn from their evil, wicked ways and repent of their sins. The ungodly will not keep God's commandments, will not call on the name of Jesus; there is no testimony of the Lord in them. Revelation 14:12 (NIV) says, "This calls for patient endurance on the part of the people of God who keep his commands and remain faithful to Jesus."

We see people all the time saying they believe in God, but they know nothing about Him and have no relationship with Him or His Son or His Word. It's because they do not care. They may have been raised in a religious church or just a building, full of spiritually dead people, with human-made rules and laws that do not bring them closer to Jesus. Looks good, sounds good, but there is no Spirit of God moving inside them, repairing their broken, dead parts . Most of the time, if someone goes to a church like this, they fall away in time or do not seem to grow spiritually in Christ. There is no power of the Holy Spirit there; find a better place to worship. If you think your pastor is not preaching total truth from God's Word, find a better pastor.

Liberal mainstream churches are all over now; the news media, Hollywood elites, and leftist socialist politicians helped set this up. Soon the Republicans will merge with the left out of fear, hate, and ungodly lies. The lies started in the Garden of Eden a long time ago and crept into the fabric of the world we live in. Some things that God hates and calls sin are called okay in certain churches. Revelation 2:4–5 (NIV) says, "Yet I hold this against you: You have forsaken the love you had at first. Consider how far you have fallen! Repent and do the things you did at first. If you do not repent, I will come to you and remove your lammpstant from its place." The Lord puts down most of the churches in the last days, out of seven churches the Lord finds favor in one church.

We can already see that laws are being changed to silence Christians and churches speaking God's truth, and lots of feel-good churches are conforming to the watered-down worldly version of God's Word. I believe there will be a Sunday law, taking away God's Fourth Commandment to keep the Sabbath Day holy. You can water down His book, but you cannot water down the Holy Spirit working inside His people. I also believe that laws will be made, enforcing bookstores to censor God's truth before selling it to the public. God's Word will be treated like a porn magazine. This is what the socialist, communist reign of the Antichrist, the beast, will look like. We can see it in Washington and around the world right now. It looks like the leftist liberal globalists are winning this battle, until Jesus comes back.

Remember, this has been going on for thousands of years, moving away from the truth of the light, closer to darkness. This started from the beginning of time. God and His Word is so strong, it always finds its way to His people to give light to the path of truth, leading to the Father Creator. Do not be like the ungodly, who would rather believe lies than the truth. In the end days, God sends them a powerful delusion (2 Thessalonians 2:11–12 (NIV)).

The end of the age is here. Jesus said the Gospel has to go out to all four corners of the earth; this has to happen before He returns. This has already happened. Other prophets in God's Word have said things like knowledge will increase in the end days; read Daniel 12:4 (NIV). Think of this: People rode horses for thousands of years, and times have changed dramatically in the past hundred years or so. I say the computer age is the knowledge increase the Lord was talking about in the end-times.

There's another prophecy we can see in our day: The Lord said He would scatter the Jewish people around the world for rejecting Jesus. In the end-times, He will bring them back to the land He gave their forefathers thousands of years ago, the land of Israel. The Jewish people would go to war against the occupiers.

After the Jewish people were taken away and scattered around the world, like God said would happen, other Middle Eastern tribes took possession of Israel. The Jewish people would have to fight to get the land back. In 1948, they did just that, and now, a prophecy can be fulfilled. In 1967, the Six-Day War was documented as a miracle battle. Israel was outnumbered ten to one with tanks and military might, but what the enemies of God's people did not think would happen, happened. God stepped in and helped the Jewish people win the war. Six days of war, then the Lord rested on the seventh day, like when He created the universe and planets. This is a fact and is documented by personal testimonies about the Six-Day War being an act of God. God sent the enemies of Israel a delusion of a massive Jewish army coming at them, and they ran for their lives.

God of Israel, the Father of Abraham, Isaac, and Jacob, said He would turn the desert land of Israel into a paradise, with fruit, trees, water, and all kinds of blessings to feed the people. Before the return of Jesus, their Savior, another prophecy would be the destruction of the original temple of God. Not one stone would be left on top of another, Jesus said. Seventy years after His resurrection, Rome destroyed the temple in Jerusalem and took complete control of the land.

Prophecy says the temple would be rebuilt one final time before Jesus comes back for His church and stomps on the head of evil, for the third and final war. As we speak, the new temple is being built, the stage is being set for the final world conflict, and the Lord's plan is coming to pass. When you study God's Word, you begin to understand that the Jews have a part to play in history. It is important to know that we can look at Israel to see where we are in time. The promise of eternal life was passed down to the new covenant church. The new covenant church is saved by mercy, grace, love, and faith in the blood shed on the cross of Christ, not by works of keeping the laws of God. Paul said the laws of God are good and true, but that is not what saves you.

Thank God, because no person can keep the laws perfectly. We have a perfect salvation in putting our faith in the finished work of Jesus alone, our King.

Because of publishing rules, parts of my documents had to be blotted out to protect people's privacy. I am hoping this does not take away the sting, the bang, the pow of it all. I hope to keep the unbelievable factors and proofs alive in my testimony. Let the Spirit of Jesus have freedom to move in your hearts. Thank you for understanding.

Let the story begin.

- 1 -
THE GREAT HUNTER, JESUS

"The Great Hunter Jesus"

We live in a supernatural world, hunting for truth, and feeding our spirit to stay alive while trying to understand life in general.

There is a divine code, a fingerprint left by God in our everyday life, things only the Creator God can do. It is there if you are looking to discover it.

Dreams, visions, and miracles are all around us, so seek them out, and you will find.

It has been said that you cannot teach an old dog new tricks. I hope you do not believe that.

Jesus said to have faith as a little child so you can believe His truths. Many people today do not believe God is working actively in the lives of others, but He is.

The Lord does leave His fingerprint. My testimony is harder to believe, because it's not like any other testimony. Even with proof, some people still won't believe in the power of God; they won't believe that He would save me. Unbelief is a direct result of

1

lies from people, rip-offs, scams, and hate from this dark world. That is understandable; just do not let it stop your miracles and blessings from coming.

A couple of my miracles are like the miracles you see in the Bible, like the stone tablets the Lord gave to Moses, written by the finger of God for all to see with their eyes and to believe; the Ten Commandments were written with God's finger, not human hands.

In the Bible, Jesus tells people to become like children. Let yourself come to a place where you can believe God is present, actively working on your behalf. He is calling us to believe in His many ways. He speaks to us. He may speak to you in a completely different way from how He speaks to me. The Lord uses whatever He wants to draw us to Himself. You might be by the seashore or standing by a river, and the sound of the water may speak to your heart in a way you cannot explain. But you know it is moving you.

The wind might start to blow, and the sound rushing through the trees begins to soften you up in your spirit; you cannot explain it, but your spirit knows it is speaking to you. Our Lord will speak to you listen and believe. When I read the Bible, the Lord speaks loud and clear to me. There is no guessing: He is telling us His story and is calling us to Himself. You will see in my testimony that the Lord used a number, 1945, to call me to Himself, and His voice was loud and clear. God told me to save certain documents because He was doing something in me, through me. This is why I saved what I did and wrote this book. I have worked on cars and motorcycles my whole life; I never thought I would write a book or have a ministry. If you belong to Jesus, you have a ministry, whether you minister out of your home, on the internet, at a coffee shop in town, or walking the streets of your salvation.

After learning about the darkness and seeing how evil works against the light, you will find it easier to hear the truth. I understand and can see why so many people stay away from the light of God's truths. If you do not already understand what I am talking about, I hope that after reading this book, you will.

After learning and understanding the truth of the blood shed on the cross of Christ, you will be attacked in different ways—sometimes suddenly, sometimes slowly and deeply. Evil powers often use family and friends, so be ready to fight a supernatural battle. Learning how to fight evil and hold on to God's truths is important, as you will use these weapons in spiritual warfare.

Satan, the great thief, liar, and deceiver, will try and take the truth away from you so you cannot share it or live by it. Hold on tight, and remember: if you feel it slipping away, ask the Lord to help you hold on. That is what I do.

Another great truth from the Word of God is that if you don't know what to pray for, you can ask the Lord what to pray for.

I wish I had taught my kids more about God as they were growing up, but because it took me so long to discover for myself, I missed the opportunity when they were young. I hope this testimony can make up for my shortcomings in my spiritual past.

- 2 -
MY DREAM CHAPTER

I had a dream about five years ago, and it was the most peaceful, beautiful-sounding dream I've ever had. In my dream, I heard a song coming from all around me, like from heaven, vibrating through all things. And there was only one word in this song: the word was Jesus. Yet the song never ended, and the one word went on and on and on, with no beginning and no end. "Jesus" was not repeated over and over—it was one word, spoken one time, which never ended. That is the best way to explain it.

Time and space were not as we know it in the natural world. I looked up to the sky, and it was beautiful, a soft orange and red, like a sunset. But there was no sun; the word was the light of what I could see. The cross of Christ was above me in the sky. Heavenly voices were all singing a beautiful, angelic melody. It felt like all Creation had joined in on the song of praise and worship. It was like every kind of instrument playing the same song as one. I felt it was becoming a part of me, or I was becoming a part of this song, permeating from within, and for me, it was a new song.

I felt like I was drifting upwards to the cross, and only the song mattered. I had no awareness of the earth. Time and space were coming together as one. Nothing else mattered but that Jesus was King. The Creator was being worshipped in song. The Word was in charge of life at that moment. God's everlasting song of love, forgiveness, mercy, grace, and redemption was complete.

Through that one word, Jesus told the whole story in the song. That is what I felt. I knew all Creation in one moment was under the power of His love. The sound of the song was everything to all things in His Creation. There was no room for evil. Eternal, everlasting peace and happiness were all there was, no darkness, and the love was the light; being with Him was life everlasting. I could not see Him in human form, but I knew who He was and is to come. I have never felt so much perfect love in harmony with just one Word.

That is the best way I can describe the sound of the song and what I heard and saw. It seemed to last forever, like there was no time; nothing else mattered but the song, and everything that was and is, was under Him; no beginning or end. The cross and beautiful sounds of the song were all that was left to see, hear, and feel. The song was the binding force that held all things together in God's Kingdom. I think it was like being in heaven; nothing was made with human hands. I had a feeling of the fullness of God's glory and love, where everything became one with the Creator.

- 3 -
NOT RELIGION, RELATIONSHIP

"Shield of Faith"

America is one of many countries spreading the Gospel of Christ. The devil hates that. And so right now, we see a great falling away from truth all around the world, not just in America. Time is very short. I hope it is not too late to shed light on what is happening, so more people can turn from sin to Jesus for eternal life in this dark world.

> Your Word is a lamp to my feet and a light for my path. (Psalm 119:105 (NIV))

I am not talking about religion here. I am not a religious person. I am talking about a personal relationship with God, Jesus. There is a difference; religion is like a job, day after day, but a personal relationship with God changes your life and lasts to the end of time. A relationship with God is getting up every day, every moment of time, wondering what He is going to do next, or whom He leads to you to tell about Him. It is exciting knowing that He is going to help you achieve your goals in life, opening doors for you.

More mysteries of God's Word are in the open, being revealed now like never before.

Do you need proof God is real? The Lord gave me the proof that convinced me to believe He is.

I have the proof. God is actively searching out people who will believe Him as the Lord to save them. I believe the documents I saved thirty years ago are proof of God's ability to do miracles and draw people to Himself. Thank God for His love, power, mercy, and saving grace; the Lord does whatever He wants, not being limited to time or space or matter. God gave me some modern-day proofs to show His awesomeness. Some people will see the miracles and believe; others will not. Only the Lord can open their minds to see and believe. Jesus said bless the man who sees and believes, and bless the man who does not see and believes.

Spiritual blindness is real; the god of this world, Satan, doesn't want anyone to see the truths, the power, the love, or the mercies God has for us.

God is still doing unbelievable things in today's world. Our Creator from the past and the revealer of today into the future has never left the building.

The Old Testament writers in the Bible stopped writing, and there was four hundred years of silence, then Jesus was born in the flesh to finish the plan of salvation.

The children of Israel were in bondage in Egypt for four hundred years; they prayed and cried out to their Lord God, Jehovah, God of Israel, Father of Abraham, Isaac, and Jacob, to save them from bondage in Egypt. Then Moses was sent in by God to lead them out of bondage; it is always on the Lord's time, not ours.

If you study the Bible correctly, it proves itself to be true; God knows the future from the end to the beginning of time, thousands of years in advance, not just in one lifetime.

Right now, I am plowing the ground before I plant more seeds of truth.

The Word of God, the Bible, became flesh. God reached out to humanity, became a man (John 1:14 (NIV)), and walked among us. A story without end.

God is mysterious; I see His hand in the Bible using people, angels, animals, and other things to do His will. There are no limits to what He will do for one person, tribe, or nation. He brings them up. And He brings them down if and when He wants to. He gives peace. He can take peace away (Jeremiah 16:5 (NIV)).

God is not the god of fast-food orders or the god to riches, unless it be His will.

People who understand the will of God and His plan of salvation can walk their life in faith, knowing we belong to Jesus, name above all other names.

It takes a hunger inside to want to study His Word. Take time to know more about God's plan for people; we should all care about that. If you do not have a hunger to study His Word, ask the Lord for it, and He will give it to you. Out of thousands of prophecies in the Bible, all but a couple have come to pass; there is no other person, book, or religion that has a plan from start to finish of a salvation plan for humankind.

The Lord provides a way to get around and or to overcome our short comings, thank God.

I've spent over thirty years saving unbelievable things from God, and these documents prove I am not hallucinating. I believe it's God working in me, through me, for me; I am glorifying God here, not me. He deserves it. Without Him, I cannot do anything.

I am going to let it shine. The cross of Christ is on your table today.

It is not easy to keep walking a straight line every day; I walk by faith.

God can leave a kind of fingerprint in different ways for us. You will see it in your life and the lives of others, if you look for it. He gives us knowledge of His being alive, actively working on earth; He and the angels never sleep. God gives us experiences we can never forget; we get to see supernatural experiences with our spiritual eyes and ears. If you are watching, sometimes the Lord will get you to stop and look at what He is doing in the moment. For example, I was working on a car, and the Lord told me to stop and look. I stopped what I was doing, looked to my left, and about a hundred feet from me, my cat was walking down the sidewalk.

I said, "Yes, Lord; that's my cat walking."

The Lord said, "Wait and watch."

My cat reached up with his claw, pulled down a rose, and smelled it. Awesome. You might say, so what? For me, there were two things going on; it was a beautiful act in nature, and I was listening to God, hearing His voice at that moment, and being obedient to His voice. Be obedient in the small things as we should in the bigger things as we grow in Him.

I will always be in learning mode with the Lord until the end; no one can know everything about God. Our brains cannot hold that much, but we should strive for His perfection, moment by moment.

Only God has the power over matter, time, and space. The Lord does give us glimpses of everything in life as we need to know it. You could say the Lord holds our hand all along the way, even when we do not know or feel it.

At some point in our salvation plan, God gives us a new heart. You need a new heart because your old heart has been corrupted with lies and disease from the world. With a new heart, you can see, feel, and hear Him, and what is around you in the world, better. We should share God's truth back to this dying, lost world because we are overflowing with what He is giving us.

It is important to learn as much as we can about God's truths; we are children of God, and there are evil enemies of His children. Jesus said count the cost of following

Him. The world hated Him; they will hate you. Spiritual warfare will happen; the Word of God is like a double-edged sword, so use it (Hebrews 4:12 (NIV)). Knowing as much scripture as you can is a weapon against evil people and evil spirits. The Word of God helps overcome sin and battle evil. There also is power in the blood of Jesus. Knowing this is important.

There are still many mysteries of God, His Word, and what He is doing in us, through us, and around us.

Only God could execute such a perfect plan for the world.

I want this story to be easy to read, with no big words; a child could read it. Without Jesus, there is no story, and I am just another number in this world like you.

I always knew there was something in me, bigger than me, speaking to my inner self. It took a lot of years to see the plan for my life; God's not finished with me yet. There is more to His plan; it is unfolding. Yes, I am saved, but things are still being worked out in my destiny.

So you also know the Lord gives us blessings, and He holds back blessings. Sometimes, we stray away from His plan, not knowing how far we have gone. And we miss out on things, so stay close to Jesus. Do not miss out on what He has for you, your family, friends, and people you have not even met yet.

- 4 -
YOUNG BOY

At a young age, I could tell that my dreams meant more than I knew; they were guiding me. I know now some dreams are not about good things, and evil can attack us while we sleep. It is important to know that friends and family members you dream about can have dreams about you; they could be good or bad dreams, moving them away from you or closer to you.

For example, one of my daughters said, "Dad, I had an ugly dream the other night." I asked her what it was.

She said I snapped the neck of her son, my grandson.

Wow, I thought. *What could this mean?* I had been trying to help her understand God and get closer to Jesus, so I came to the conclusion that evil was actively working to put doubt in her mind about me.

I'm not sure every time I think God or His angels speak to me, but I'd like to think I know most of the time, but we do have selective hearing at times, don't we?

As a young boy, when my relationship started with God, I didn't know anything about Him or religion or church people, but I just knew God and His angels were watching me. I tried to get God to reveal Himself to me by asking Him to do things. Like I wanted candy, chocolate, something good to eat, or a toy I could play with, so I'd ask Him to deliver it, but He never did magic for me like that. I still asked because I am human, and we have minds like that. That is how most of us think, especially at a young age. God is not that kind of God. He does not come out of a bottle when we rub it and go away when we think He isn't needed.

As I got older, my relationship with the Lord started to take shape; it became clearer to me every moment, every year. I started saving things at a young age because I heard a voice in my mind telling me to. I know now that it was the Spirit of God asking me to save certain things, to put stuff away in a safe place for the future, knowing someday it would add up to something I could understand. I had faith in that.

I was nineteen when I realized a number, 1945, started to repeat itself to me and speak to my spiritual self.

I eventually surrendered to Jesus on November 13, 1997. God used a number to fish me out of the scum of the earth. After surrendering to Him, I asked God, "What would You have of me? Why are You doing this to me?"

He said to put the things He had given me together, along with my experiences and personal relationship with Him, and write it into a book. It would be my testimony of how I came to know Who God is. He said to show the world how He got me to believe in His awesome power, mercies, and love, and explain that He is alive, actively working on my behalf to bring me home to Himself one day.

By faith, I listened year after year. Wow, how awesome He is. It took thirty-seven years to get to that day of complete surrender and almost another thirty years to finish writing my testimony.

Even in today's world, God will do the unbelievable; He is still in the miracle and saving souls business.

When I grew up, my family never went to church. My parents didn't go to church. I thought the Bible was just another book someone wrote, and Jesus was Santa Claus's baby. I am not kidding; I did not know anything about Jesus or religion. After finding out Santa Claus, the reindeer, and the little elves were fake, then the baby Jesus Christmas story was fake to me too.

Growing up thinking Jesus was a fake story kept me from the truth for quite some time. Anytime someone approached me as I was getting older to tell me about Jesus, I would just laugh in their face. I wondered how people could still believe in Santa Claus and his baby Jesus; it was beyond me. I was thirty-seven years old before I knew Jesus was in the Bible. Think about that for a minute. I thought Jesus was Santa Claus's baby until I was thirty-seven years old. Satan had me right where he wanted me: lost in lies, like fake news.

I tried to write for years, but every time I sat down to write, I could not get past the first couple pages because there was always something I had to do or fix: car, truck, bike, work, a party to go to, girls, a wife, kids, drugs. They all stopped me from finishing my story. I was sure at least 20 per cent of this stopping me was the evil powers of this world, right. It could not have been because I was too busy working, living, smoking pot, drinking, fighting in the bars, living in the fast lane. You think? It took Noah a hundred years to build the ark. Okay, it was a very big ark, and he did a lot of drinking.

I wish I had written this a long time ago. You will soon find out how unusually powerful my testimony is. I have only read of miracle stories like mine in the Bible, where every word can be a supernatural experience.

It took me thirty-seven years to believe in the Bible. And it will take a lifetime of study to understand what God's Word means. I always believed strongly in the supernatural mysteries of the world and that there was a God. But did not really know His name or who He was.

- 5 -
DISCERNING THE SPIRITS

Did you know singing and whistling to yourself can be a form of worship to God? Because you are happy, and you did not even know you were doing it. It is easy, and it is free. Worship God every moment; it changes lives, and the Lord created us to worship Him for His good pleasure.

The devil wants to be worshipped too; this is another reason war broke out in heaven with the angels. And on earth, like it or not, we are stuck in the middle of this spiritual conflict of good and evil. For the most part, the battle is over our souls, another important thing to understand. This war started long ago in ancient times in heaven. Some people act evil simply because they think it is cool, like a fad, or it is a bad choice they make. By nature, all people are sinners, and some people are possessed by demons. Other people know the difference between good and evil, and turn to the good light of truth of the Lord, because God's love for them is stronger than the darkness working around them.

In the garden, Adam and Eve disobeyed God, and that was a sin, because they were fooled with Satan's strongest tool in his toolbox: lies that kill us. The devil wants to separate all of us from God. Sin can separate us, and separation from God is death. I want everyone to know that Adam and Eve did not die because of poison in the fruit; it was because they disobeyed God, and He separated from them. They began the aging process and died.

Every person has a spiritual side to discover at some point. The sooner you discover this, the better it is, and the sooner you grow in Jesus. He is our supernatural God; see Him as all-knowing and all powerful, at all times. Jesus has no beginning and no end. He is the Omega.

I am not a college professor; far, far, far from that, although I spent a large part of my life collecting proof of my experiences, asking questions, praying, being open to the unbelievable supernatural world we live in, and documenting what I experienced. At a young age, I had a hunger to figure out if God was real, and then God showed Himself to me a couple different times, not in human form, but in different ways. God asked me to read the Bible a couple times through the years. I tried but just could not understand it. Before discovering the scripture as truth, I thought it was a book some guy wrote about God a long time ago.

After surrendering to God and reading His Word, the Lord showed me His truths. I found the Bible to be true. Reading the Bible is the best way to discover Who God really is, in a fuller way. I realize some of you readers know God already. That is good. Amen.

"Vines of Life"

- 6 -
THREE BUILDING BLOCKS FOR SPIRITUAL GROWTH

At this point in my story, I am trying to show people who do not know Jesus that the Word of God is worth reading; it reveals God's nature and His salvation plan.

You should have three main building blocks in your life.

Block 1 is the heavenly Father, block 2 is the Son, and block 3 is the Holy Spirit. There are many more dimensions, parallels, and combinations of realities in those three things. In other words, without the first three building blocks in your life, you could be colder, dryer, darker, and alone. Like stagnant, stinky water in a dung storm of darkness, drying up without God, endlessly wandering without hope of anything more in life.

Life is more fulfilling with the Word of God, Jesus, the Bible, and all His promises. Blessings will come as you grow in the knowledge of Him and are adopted into His family by faith.

Building a relationship with God is a lifetime commitment, but it gets better as you go. Do not worry. He already did the hard, painful work. It is not about how much money you give to the church or how rich you can get. God's Word said a blood sacrifice is needed to take away our sins. The sin debt was to be paid for with blood, blood of the Lamb of God, perfect in all its ways. After believing and receiving the free gift of eternal life, by the power of the crucified Christ on the cross, you are in.

The fear of the Lord is the beginning of the knowledge of your salvation. This truth will set you free. The fear of the Lord is not fear like He is going to kill you; it means you are in awe of His majesty, His all-knowing power, and His love over all things. It's kind of like children fear their parents, but they know they love them. Most parents, I believe, want the best for their kids, so they teach them with a strong hand. If you never had parents like that, you'll have to imagine it.

In the book of Genesis, after Adam and Eve ate from the forbidden tree, they were hiding from God in the garden. God called out to Adam, "Where are you?" The Lord knew where they were; He wanted them to step out into the open, to look them in the eyes and speak with them.

He had His reasons. Remember, God knows the end before the beginning, so He was not surprised by what happened. At times, the Word of God can be hard to understand. If I read something in scripture and don't understand it, I know now to pray for understanding. And if I still don't understand it, I come to the conclusion it is not for me to understand at that time. I may understand it later, because there are things I did not understand in the past, but today I do. God may wait till it is time to show you something or until you are ready to understand; some things are better not to know. The more you learn, the more you are accountable for. Some people cannot understand that; it is part of how big God, Creator of all things, is. He is perfect in all His ways; He knows what is best. Trust Him and His ways.

All of creation is under His all-knowing power, at the same time.

People are like blades of grass in this universe of time to God. Our heavenly Father still wants to see us in the open; there's no reason to hide. He is the God of life and love.

We can walk with God in the gardens of life again because Jesus paved the way with His blood.

Jesus is the master fisher and hunter of men. When you see God at work, you realize that only God has the power to do such things. He moves in answering prayers and other things that are in His will. At times, He does the unthinkable to get us to look. He does things people cannot do so we can see how awesome He is. That is another way you know it is Him working.

When you fall on the rock, you're broken; if the rock falls on you, you are crushed. God will use whatever works to draw His children back to Himself.

- 7 -

MY MIRACLE NUMBER: 1945

I have saved seven documents from God. Keep in mind, it is not always what I or we see that convinces us it is the Lord working on our behalf. It can be that feeling inside stirring us up. Most messages I get from God come with a spoken word in my spiritual self, with the experience and documents.

Long before I was born, an envelope with my name on it and dated September 17, 1945, was put in a box and forgotten about for years (I was born in 1959). When my brother Joe got married, his wife had a couple of her grandma's boxes in their garage. One of those boxes had this envelope. If that did not happen, I never would have found the envelope. I believe it was for me, from God.

No one wanted this envelope; it was one of those things that got lost in time. Written on the envelope was "Ted's first haircut by Uncle Buster, September 17, 1945." God had another plan for this envelope after Ted grew up. From the ashes of time, headed for the garbage can, it would become my letter from God. An envelope to me, my name on it, headed for the future with a word of knowledge from God. About forty years later, I found it.

God is the only one who could set something like this up. He made sure I found the envelope with the four-digit code, 1945. It was not just my name; it was the number along with my first name and a spoken Word. It was created in the past. It is in the present now. And it will go into the future, telling how God can work in a person's life. Even after you read this, when God does things, it could live on in time, a story without end, kind of like the Bible.

God called out my name: "Buster! Where are you?" I was born in 1959. There is a mystery in this envelope story, dated 1945, with Buster written on it. I did not think of this or do this by myself; really, I could not have kept this up for forty years hearing, seeing, saving, and telling people about it. Most of my family and friends thought I was trying to be funny; some still do, but I was not playing a game. I know this does not make sense to you yet, but it will.

Every time the number would come up, it would move me inside and speak to me.

Seeing that number over the years set me up to change my life. That is another miracle. It is not just how the number was popping in on me and speaking; it is what it was doing to me too. It took years before I completely understood how the number was being used. Little by little, my faith in God was being built on a personal relationship, on solid ground.

The first time God gave me something, I believed it was Him, and I believed every time after that. Sure, there are times I see the number and know it was not from God. I did not save everything with 1945, but only if it came with a message from God for me. I would save it if I could. I know the difference from normal everyday TV programs or if I saw the number in a book or somewhere on a sign.

People have asked me, "How do you know when it is God speaking to you?"

Most of the time, you just know, and He has a still small voice that Satan cannot duplicate, although the devil does try to sound like God to throw you off. Satan tries to imitate God.

Sometimes, you have to believe by faith when words of knowledge come from God. It's easy for me to see or hear the Spirit of God speak to me now. It can be overwhelming when God is moving you to a place to speak to you. Angels are God's messengers in the spirit realm. Being connected to Jesus in the spirit is being with God or having a supernatural experience. When you feel God moving, that is like Him speaking to you. Like at church, you know it's God communicating through someone preaching His Word. This is part of God's plan.

The Bible says, by the hearing of the Word of God, the Gospel of Jesus being preached leads people to their salvation. That is not the only way God leads you to Himself but the most popular. Take King David or Moses in the Old Testament; the Gospel of Jesus had not come yet. But it did not stop God from using them to put His salvation plan into play.

If you have evil thoughts or feelings, they are not from God. If they are true and good, they are from God. This is another way to know the Lord may be giving you some good knowledge. We need those conversations in the spirit, and we need that relationship with Jesus to help keep us strong.

The three members of the Trinity helped me put this book together for people to see: the Father, Son, and Holy Spirit.

It turns out that when you know what you know that you know, that's a good thing.

- 8 -

GOD BLESSES AMERICA, FOR NOW

We are a free nation of people; it has nothing to do with religion. Who does not want freedom and peace? America has come a long way together as a mix of people and tribes and beliefs; we see better now how life is unfolding in history. What would this land look like if China, Russia, Iran, or Germany invaded five hundred years ago, or even today? Thankfully, it was founded on godly principles. God bless America. Communism could be in control. No freedoms in Christ, that is for sure.

Nations still grab territory today, killing everyone who gets in their way. America is the best place in the world to live free under God. Our Constitution and the Bible are the best documents we have as a people in a dying world.

The Lord brings nations up, and He brings nations down. You'll understand that, if you believe in the Word of God, the Bible.

We live in a world of supernatural dimensions, combinations of religions, colors, dreams, tribes, sounds, shapes, smells, numbers, codes, yes, and lies. Finding the truth nowadays is not easy. Every person is born a sinner, by nature.

I also believe the mark of the beast is not just a number, described in the Bible as 666; it stands for a system of death. Saying yes to this system of death is taking the mark of the beast. It is a spiritual choice we make inside our souls, our spiritual selves. We all make that choice at some point in our lives, and at that moment, we get our mark. God marks His children as saved when we say yes to Jesus. We know at that point we have His mark, the seal of life by the Lord. What a good thing that is, and it's free.

I do not think most people would get into a line for their mark from the beast. If people knew that is what it was, they would not take it. Some get tricked or forced through lies. The Antichrists use work, food, money, fame, sex, and drugs to fool you. I do not think people will get into a long line knowing they are going to get marked 666 from the beast. But the Bible does say the mark of the beast will be put on our forehead or our right hand. Everyone must choose who they will serve, who is their

God. At some point, the Lord will ask them who they will serve: the light of the truth, or the darkness of lies and death.

Life is not a random chance of the draw.

People came from the dust of the earth, and to dust our bodies will return. That is another connection we have to the land.

"Winds of Change"

- 9 -
GOD MOVES US INTO HIS PLAN

Our memories are like spider webs, intertwined and woven in this vast universe of life. Vibrating matter, thoughts, music, animal sounds, the wind, rain, thunder, all of creation, the sound of running water or crashing waves all vibrate at different levels and move us closer to God's purpose. No one can hide from it. From the beginning of time, everything is in motion, connected and moving into a planned outcome called our future.

If you want to get to heaven, just call on the name of Jesus.

Many tribes and bands of people have nothing left of their history; it's lost to time. Some people still alive today tell their stories of survival, wars, and tribulations through time, their beliefs, and their gods. The God of Israel has stood up to the test of time. The Israelites wrote documents about their relationship with God and the history of their people for thousands of years. All part of God's plan. Have you ever wondered why so many countries and people hate the Jews and Israel? The Bible tells us that in the end days, the whole world will come up against Israel. People who hate Jews are lost without the true God. God's foretold plan will come to pass. Israel is a part of the plan; it always has been. And trust me, the world has been watching this plan unfold for thousands of years. Many people still do not believe in the God of Israel. That is sad.

People say, "I do not believe in God." But they blame God for all the bad things that happened to them or the bad choices they made in life, right? But if you do not believe in God, how can you blame Him for the bad stuff that happens?

Rome ruled the world for a long time with their gods and system of death, their rules and laws over the people. When Jesus was born, Rome controlled most of the world. At that time, Roman officials required all the people to register in the town of their birth.

The name of His father, Joseph, His mother, Mary, and baby Jesus, Himself, was documented for all to see by the Romans. The name of Jesus is the name above all other names on earth and in heaven.

The Romans did not always kill people on a cross. They started crucifying people just a few years before Jesus was born; it had to happen for God's Word to come true. Jewish people were very meticulous about documenting their dreams, visions, and prophecies, even though God's prophets were normally put to death because the leaders did not want to hear the truth if it was against them. Does this sound like anyone you know in today's world?

The Jewish people took good care of their documents from their God: history of families, miracles, events, wars, victories and losses, and the promises of their God, Jehovah, Father God of Abraham, Isaac, and Jacob. History unfolded right before their eyes. Back in those days, if you lied about something and got caught, they would kill you. Even if it was the truth, you could be killed right on the spot. So the amount of lies was limited to very few. If it came to a bigger deal, like when Jesus said, "I am God," plan on being put to death.

We understand lots of mysteries nowadays because we have scriptures. A thousand years ago, people could not understand much of God's Word, because it is beyond their ability. People had to advance into the technology age to understand what some things in scripture were talking about for the end-times, our coming future.

The timing is always important in understanding God's Word. Only if God opens our eyes for us to see can we understand His truths in His Word, the Bible. We get inside information from the Spirit of God if He wants us to know something. For the most part, the Bible has everything we need to be saved. We get understanding and the things we need to know about heaven and earth.

We can now use computers and the web to make Bible studies faster, answering questions and making it easier to see God's work and His plan unfolding.

After studying the Bible, I discovered my inner self was alive and growing. What the Lord was showing me never seemed to end. For some reason, I thought after I surrendered to Jesus, the number 1945 thing would stop. I am still getting the number and things that show me how awesome He is. The Lord is always full of surprises. If you watch closely, you can see Him at work in my life.

This book is not just another unbelievable story. After you get the whole picture, I hope the truth spreads faster than wildfire so more lives will be saved.

For many years, I asked God to reveal Himself openly to me, saying, "Who are You? Speak to me. Give me a sign."

Most people want a sign from God. But the sign God gives you may not be the sign you are looking for. The Bible says asking God for signs is not a good thing. The Bible has the biggest signs of all; it reveals everything we need to know about how to live and how to see the Father, Son, and Holy Ghost. To me, the Bible is like the Lord's fingerprint of His love story to humanity.

Say you are at a casino, gambling; you think, *Oh, Lord, let me win so I can help everyone. I will not gamble any more for a while if I win big.*

We've all done this, or close to it: "Let me win this raffle, drawing, or bingo game. I need this car. I want that Harley." You have a feeling God is watching you, right? Or you hope He is there to help. LOL.

Little by little, day by day, year after year, God showed Himself with a strong hand in my life. Kind, loving, and mysterious at the same time, gentle as a lamb in many different ways, calling me to Himself.

- 10 -
DRUNK ON THE SPIRIT OF GOD

The first miracle I want to share is how I came from being a thief, liar, scoundrel, and scum bucket, blind, deaf, and spiritually dead. Well, maybe not a scum bucket, but close. Lost in a dying world, I was an unrepentant sinner, blind to the marvelous light of the truth of Jesus; my salvation in Jesus is my greatest miracle. The world is a safer place because of me surrendering to Jesus. That is my first miracle of all. If you cannot see that, you cannot see anything.

A relationship, not a religion.

I never want to bow down to organized religions. I do not believe in 80 percent of temples, churches, fortune-tellers, or organized groups of human theologies of Who God is or what His Word means to them.

I came to the Lord because God drew me to Himself, not by a church of any denomination telling me what to believe or how to believe it. I was not indoctrinated by my family, so when the Lord picked me up, it was easier to believe His truths, not human lies. I will not try to get anyone to join a church of doctrines, demons, or devils for your money, free sex, or labor.

I found out the word *religion* is used in different ways by different people. Religion can be dangerous. It can also help lead people to Jesus and get saved.

I am involved in an in-depth study of what is real and what is true, good angels and bad angels in the supernatural world; my studies have been mostly in the Harvard school of hard knocks: hand-to-hand combat on dirt or grass, in bars or houses, and on concrete. Now I am drunk on the Spirit of God, as much as possible.

Religion can be like dope to some people. It has played a part in the history of humanity from the beginning of documented time.

People have been writing their thoughts and dreams down for thousands of years. They documented things on rocks, copper, grass, paper, clay, leather, wood, all kinds of stuff. Keeping the thoughts, memories, and history of people alive and passing them down for all generations, they must be important, right? From the beginning of time, people like you and me have searched out what truth means to us. Most of us know we have a spiritual side.

Some people cannot put their finger on it, yet we all know there is something supernatural going on, and it is alive, actively working things out in more than one dimension, behind the curtains of life's mysteries.

God's plan is to get back what was lost in the garden. One of the most important things in His plan is that every person is saved.

Some people have a stronger desire to search out spiritual things than others. The Bible says each and every person has a measure of faith put in them by God, a hunger to search for the Creator. The Lord did that to be fair, so nobody can say they never had a chance to look for God when their judgment day comes.

At a young age, my mind was easily corrupted with fake information; I wanted candy. I tried to make candy, soda pop, and stuff with my mind; I thought I had those powers. I never could do that kind of magic, of course. I still believed there was a God, and with practice, I thought I could make candy appear. I thought I was a normal kid. I watched a lot of TV, and my small mind was open to the possibilities of what could be true.

Catching up with the invisible God takes time and determination; you have to pray and have a hunger to know Him.

You should know the truth before you get to heaven. I believe God wants to tell everyone His story in a personal way from the Bible.

Eternal life, I am sure everyone would agree, is worth more than Hollywood, Super Bowl Sunday, and all the silver and gold in the world. Remember, God wants to get to know you more than you may want to know Him. He has a good reason for aggressively revealing Himself to you.

Thinking back, I remember my third grade teacher saying to me, "Buster, someday I think you may be a writer," because of a story I wrote in class. Funny how that is the only thing I remember in the first six years of school. I do remember going to the principal's office for being bad. I found out if you go there, it is paddle time. In those days, kids got whacked if they were bad.

I went there two or three times. The principle had dozens of paddles hanging on his wall in his office. For fun, he let you pick which paddle you got whacked with. I found out in the fourth grade, they still do paddling if you are bad.

- 11 -
GOD MEANS MANY THINGS TO MANY PEOPLE

God even gave me a burning bush experience, like Moses. I will tell you about it later in my testimony.

God used a donkey to speak to Balaam in Numbers 22:28 (NIV). The Lord uses whatever He wants. I have seen it personally. Not a speaking donkey, but numbers that were speaking to me.

Angels of the Lord help people in different ways. The Lord works through angels to pass messages on to people, even in our dreams. He is actively helping us to make better choices in our lives and to warn us of danger and to help us make good choices. I had to come to a place of understanding to trust this; after a while, I did.

When I read the Bible, I can hear God's Word speaking to my heart. Study His Word. I will be repeating this all through my testimony because it is where the power of life can come from. A strong, soft voice begins to make a way into your life, without interfering with your free will, nursing you spiritually back to a healthy body and mind. Left alone in this dark world, without God, we would die without hope of eternal life.

I did not come to the Lord because I am smart or cute. I was fished out of the sea of people in the world by Jesus.

Jesus is my window of light, my hope, my burning bush, my awakening, the parting of the Red Sea, my "I saw the Light moment," the arc of my salvation, my truths, my bread and meat of life, my rivers of living water, my wine, my rock, my fortress, my King, my inspiration, my sweet fragrance, my refuge, my Father, my teacher, the anchor for my boat, my peace, my Emmanuel, my Creator, my friend, my payment for sins, my hope of life everlasting, my bridge back to the Father. Jesus is my mediator to God, and there are more, just to name a few.

Growing up, I did not go to church and learn how to pray. My mom and dad did not go to church, either. My first impressions of God were probably from watching TV. As a young boy, I remember watching a movie about Jesus dying on the cross, and I cried. I remember that. I did not understand any of it, like why He was beaten and nailed to the cross, or why He had to pay the sin debt with His blood, or why people were killing Him. Little kids just know when it is wrong.

My dad would make me and my older brother Joe fight. He beat me a lot. I remember crying, then mom would step in and stop it. I think that helped me become a better fighter, so in a way, that was a good thing because I won a lot of fights in my younger days.

My first memory of praying to God was one night, Mom and Dad were fighting, arguing at the dinner table. Mom got up and stood by the stove; I was directly across the table from Dad, and he threw a fork at her. And yup, it hit me on the top of my head. It started bleeding down my forehead. I knew not to cry because Dad got mad if we cried. Mom fixed me up. I was in the room, crying, not because the fork in my head hurt but because Dad was so mean. I asked God to make me be a nice daddy if I ever had kids; it was the first prayer I remember saying. Somehow, I knew there was a God; His voice of reason was in me, guiding me.

Looking back now, I see how all my good and bad experiences were working themselves out for the good in my life. Another miracle in this story is how ugly I was inside before God cleaned me up. I still struggle with things in my life. We all struggle with being human and the constant temptations to sin; they never end until we get glorified after the first death. The Bible says the blood of Jesus covers a multitude of sins; thank God.

- 12 -
I AM SORRY FOR MY SINS

I am very sorry to the people I hurt along the way in my life. I am not proud of a lot of things I have done. It makes me sad to think about. I am truly sorry for my past mistakes against family and people I hurt. Yes, I am guilty of many things, but getting forgiveness from Jesus gives me hope. I do realize some people will never forgive me, but that is okay. Someday, they too will be found by Jesus and ask for forgiveness, then Jesus can teach them how to forgive themselves and others like me.

When I was around seven years old, my mom bought me a thin paperback book about a Native American boy riding his horse. This was the only book from my childhood I kept. I saved it, but it got lost for many years moving around so much from town to town. Twenty years ago, I found it again. The book was dated 1945. There is more; in the end, these pieces of my puzzle fit together, making a picture that I could see, and I am doing my best to show you how it happened. Keep in mind, my testimony of the number started when I was seven years old. It is like a puzzle called "build your spiritual picture." Now, granted, I did not see the completed picture until I was thirty-seven; that is a long time to be waiting and believing it was true and from the Lord with a plan.

My brother Joe and I were fighting one time, and I finally got him to say, "I give." I cannot remember what we were fighting about. I was around eleven years old, and it was like freedom from his torture. After that, he did not mess with me much. If he got mad enough, he would try and hit me with a hammer, knife, broomstick, anything he could find. I became a fast runner, very fast.

Mom got a babysitter to watch us from time to time. She was around sixteen years old, a neighbor from three houses down. My brother and I liked kissing her. She liked it too. She showed us how to kiss better. We would take turns kissing her.

Some of the older girls in the neighborhood would pants Joe and me, grabbing at our privates. It was fun; it didn't hurt, although at first, I would scream like a girl. I was afraid. Sometimes, I thought it put a sexual curse on me. I was too young to start this kind of sex play, but kids will be kids. It did not take me long to teach girls my age to play like this. Some girls liked it, and others did not. I regret playing this game as a kid. I look back and see some of it was wrong, but it was the culture at the time.

I was a fast runner. If someone bullied me, I would punch them in the face and run like a deer. They never did catch me. I remember punching this guy in the fifth grade, and I saw him at a party in our twenties. At first glance, I wasn't sure if he was going to pay me back, but he did not hold any grudges. We had a beer, laughed, and had a good time talking about when we were kids in grammar school.

I played all the sports in school and was okay at most things. I was not learning anything in school. Mom and Dad definitely were not teachers because Joe and I both struggled in school.

When I was around ten, Mom had my sister, Beth. We moved from Concord, California, down into Clayton; it was only a couple miles away, so we kept lots of our old friends. We made more new friends in Clayton. Many people rode horses for fun; a lot of kids smoked weed and hash. There was lots of horse stables around us. I wished we could have stayed there through high school.

- 13 -

MY PARENTS DIVORCED

When I was in the seventh grade, Mom and Dad decided to divorce. It was not as bad as other divorces I heard about from my friends. It seemed okay; they did not fight over us kids, that's for sure. Dad gave Mom "Go-away money," which lasted a month or so. Dad continued to be a hard worker and successfully invested in property. He did very well for himself. He owned muffler shops and houses.

Not long after the divorce, Mom moved to Hayward, California. I was in junior high school at the time. When I was walking home the first week, I got jumped by three kids after school. I thought I was a pretty good fighter up to that point; found out I was not as good as I thought. I did have guts and a lot of heart. I started taking martial arts. I was fighting better and took some classes at a boys' club in San Leandro.

We lived near Grandpa's house for a short time. I went to junior high for one year and only got punched in the face by one guy after school. I rolled with the punch and got a bloody nose, but it did not hurt that bad. Then we moved back to Hayward, where I started high school. I wanted to play tackle football, but I was too late for trials that year. Not playing football led me to the school of hard knocks. After that, I never played ball or sports again.

By this time, my mom had a boyfriend, Paul, and after two years, they had a baby boy. Joe was not around much because he did not get along with Paul. My brother spent some time in Job Corps, a program for kids learning a trade in San Jose. Right after Jay was born, Paul moved out. I have good memories on that street from ninth to eleventh grade; a bunch of girls lived on our street. Till this day, I still have good friends from that street: Judy, Trish and her brothers Fred and John, Kathy and her sister Betty, and their brothers Hector, Ray, and Jose. There were about seven kids in that family. My friend Billy ended up in prison for murder. Some other friends were Patty, Jimmy, Joe, Roy, Rhonda, Barbara, Kitty, Tommy, Philly, and Dale. Rick and his sister, Katie, lived next door to us. Judy and her brothers and sisters lived across the street and down a couple houses; I'll always remember Judy had the nicest legs. She was cute, and her smile could melt butter. I felt a strong love for her, yet we only kissed two times. I was fifteen years old. Funny how the memory of a couple kisses stays in my mind.

Many of my friends committed suicide, all at young ages.

I still had friends in Concord. I would take BART to Concord and visit friends. While I lived in Hayward, I had a girlfriend from Concord. Chris was a wild Latino girl. She was the first girl I felt jealous of around other guys. We broke up after a year or so, and my BART trips stopped because friends and I were getting to the age of getting our license to drive.

"House on the Hill"

If we weren't driving far, we would steal a car or motorcycle to get around. That is when I entered into a stealing age. Most of my friends in Hayward were criminals. Jimmy, Tommy, Shawn, Bobby, John, Hector, and Ray were my closest friends back then. I hung out with Jimmy, Tommy, and Bobby the most, or should I say, we did the most crimes together getting high, drinking, doing LSD; we be trippin'. I am not proud of some of the things I did in my teenage years.

I really was looking to blend in and make friends, and my new friends were eager to show me how to be a thief. Snatching a purse was my initiation to their friendship. If we wanted something, we would take it from others; we broke the law for fun, stealing cars, guns, and motorcycles; selling drugs; armed robbery; burglary: We did it all. There really was not much going on inside me with God at that time. I was lost, but there was still hope for me. God is the great I AM, the great fisher of men, and in time, my criminal age would end.

In high school, I was out of control. We had drugs, we had girls, our parents weren't watching us, and we were good at lying about what we were doing. I remember Mom asking me when I was going to stop being a criminal. I told her when I turned eighteen or got busted.

I am not proud of those days; in fact, I left out a lot, because I did not want to spend lots of time on my sins. I am just showing you how far away kids can get and how strong the Lord's hand can be to bring the lost back to Himself, no matter how far they get.

My first offense was getting busted with a joint in junior high. My second offense was when I was in high school, in Hayward. I was sixteen years old. We got busted doing an armed robbery. We robbed a drive-through dairy. The cops spotted the car we were in, pulled us over, laid us out on the freeway, cuffed us, and took us to juvenile hall. I was incarcerated for two weeks for that robbery. One good thing from going to juvenile hall, I knew I did not like being locked up. I love my freedom. I kind of slowed down, that's for sure.

After that, our crime spree ended, for the most part. Even though I was stealing and breaking all kinds of laws, inside, spiritually, I felt different from my friends. Nobody I was around knew anything about Jesus or God; we were just kids.

- 14 -
FEELING DIFFERENT FROM OTHER PEOPLE

The older I got, the more different I felt. I knew I was coming to some kind of spiritual awakening, even at sixteen years old. I just did not know when it would happen. We dropped LSD in high school; that always felt spiritual. It sure felt like another dimension. Every acid trip was different, but the same enlightening of some kind would make me feel set apart from my friends. I just did not understand what, how, or why I was different spiritually.

The pages of my life were unfolding fast. I knew that someday, I was going to discover some kind of a mystery of the universe, something about God in me. It was something important, a powerful truth about Who God is and how I was part of it. It was a hunger. It is hard to explain the feeling inside me, a desire to search.

The whisper of God can be like the wind, blowing a message, a word of knowledge. So, I searched to understand; sounds, feelings, designs, patterns, colors, and dreams all went into my database in my spirit. My mind stored events in my memory card, random thoughts like a puzzle, all building my character and faith in God.

In my teens, my friends would say I wasn't normal because I talked about being psychic. They would say, "Stop talking about supernatural spiritual things like God." It was like I was so far ahead of people at a young age, I could not seem to find friends who were like me spiritually. I never was evil; at least I did not think I was. I loved animals and, for the most part, liked people. I always thought of myself as a good person, a nice person, from as far back as I could remember. As a matter of fact, after getting in fights, I felt bad about beating people up, most of the time.

I found out the man I thought was my father was not my real dad. My aunt told me Paul was my real dad. What? Yes, I was lied to for years about who my real dad was. No wonder he beat me so much. He beat me and Joe a lot. I don't think he cared whether we were his real kids or not; he was just mean and angry most of the time. I don't think he cared about either one of us, or maybe he didn't know how to show he cared, but lots of families experience this; it's nothing new.

So my little brother is my full-blooded brother; Joe and my sister are half-siblings.

At the time, I didn't really care; it did not seem to affect me. Later on, it bugged me a little because I wanted to have a dad in my life. I was a little mad at my mom about it. I finally worked it all out within myself. What bothered me the most was being lied to the first fifteen years of my life. I know now that my real dad was evil. This is disgusting and painful.

Paul moved out, and she got another boyfriend, Ted, and they moved to Minneapolis soon after hooking up, where Ted was enrolling in a vo-tech school for welding. The school lasted about two years. I didn't go with them at first. I lived with my uncle in Pleasanton, California, for eleventh grade. I really liked it there, way better than Hayward; the other kids had cars, so we didn't have to steal them to go cruising around. The people seemed nicer and had money to party.

I only got in trouble one time while I lived at my uncle's house. I was sent to juvenile hall for two weeks after using a credit card I found. I saw a purse laying on the ground, and a credit card fell out in front of me. I could not help myself. I'm not proud that I had sticky fingers. I was a kid, for goodness sake. I went to the store and bought some shoes and pants.

Sorry, I was bad. I just want you to see my life before Jesus fixed me up; the work is still ongoing. It's a never-ending process.

I started to have more spiritual experiences. I had another experience while I was in juvenile hall. It was early morning, and I was just lying there in the bed before getting up, and I had this thought to see if I could cause an earthquake. This was nothing new for me. It started at a young age, wanting to have abilities to move objects or make candy bars. I tried but was never able to.

Anyway, I wanted to exercise my mind power. I know now I cannot, that was how I would think sometimes. There is power in the mind. I tried. This is how I did it in my mind: I was outside earth's atmosphere, like astral projection in space. Don't ask me why I was thinking this. I envisioned being out in space, looking at earth, thinking how I was bringing all the planets in line; my mind was rotating in sync, in tune, and then I thought about an earthquake. I had never done that before or again.

A couple of hours later, the news on the radio said there was an earthquake in the Bay Area. I did not feel it. I was in San Leandro juvenile hall, and it is possible the quake hit before I even did what I did. I didn't know what time the quake was, but I was thinking about a quake around 5 a.m. Looking back on this now, I think I just picked up on the quake mentally and turned it into a created thing in my mind.

I say that because people have said to me, "Buster, you are making this 1945 thing up."

I say back to them, "I am not. Look at the evidence."

I realize some things I could do myself, if I tried, but there are some things going on here only God could do. That is easy to see. As you read on, you too will see the documents I saved, no person could duplicate, even if they tried. It is beyond human thinking, and this went on for thirty years. These things have meaning and power, and a word of knowledge comes at the same time as I get them. God always gives me a message and tells me to save things. So it is a combination of things that happen to move me to believe in God. There is a perfect order and depth, not to mention sound, and I got saved through it all. Hello, only God can do stuff like this. At the end of this story, you will see the beauty in it. I hope you can see the beauty and power of God in my testimony.

- 15 -
HUNTING IN SOUTH DAKOTA

The first time I ever left California, I was seventeen and flew to Minneapolis. I saw many lakes from the plane as we were coming in to land; Minnesota is called "Land of 10,000 Lakes." I was moving out there to live with my mom and Ted, who said we could go hunting together. They picked me up in Minneapolis, and we drove six hours to Veblen, a small town in South Dakota on the Sisseton Wahpeton Sioux Tribe Reservation. Ted was a member of this tribe. He and I went hunting around Peever, South Dakota, on the reservation. Later that night, we found a party up on a hill near Sisseton, and I heard stories that Chief Gabriel Renville's spirit would sit on his horse on a hill. There was a bar built in the 1930s, where I met another member of the tribe named Gloria. She and I had a good time.

After hunting a couple days, Ted, my mom, and I went back to Minneapolis. I loved Minnesota; the drinking age was eighteen, and I looked twenty-five (right; LOL). I got better at pool during those days. Ted and I would team up and play for drinks. We did well some nights, and we also got into a couple bar-room brawls. Of course, that was always fun. One night, Ted's nephew Henry was drinking with us, and we had a big brawl, ending up in the streets, another good memory. Henry had a sister Becca, who I kissed a couple times. Henry always kept a close eye on us, so Becca and I never got too close.

While living in Minnesota, I went to a tech school for mechanics. I finished a six-hundred-hour auto class course in tune-ups and brakes. Learning to be a mechanic was very helpful when working on my cars, later in life, and getting a job.

I did some boxing at the boys' club at the Native American Center. My trainer was named Bill. His brother, Steve, was a fighter too. Steve fought a famous world champ boxer a couple years later. I had one fight; I lost, but if it had been a street fight, I would have smashed him up. Three rounds went too fast. I still had lots of fight left in me; I should have let it all go and not held back. I think I had a little stage fright. I learned to let it all go; if it's a three-round fight, have no mercy, Buster.

After Ted finished his schooling, he and my mom, sister, and brother loaded up the car and truck and headed back to California. It was about a three-day drive back then. Gloria and I kept in touch.

I really was not thinking about God that much. I had one deep prayer in those days; it was that God would make me a nice daddy if I ever became a father. When we drove back to the West Coast, I was eighteen and just starting to live my life. The open road was cool; we crossed the badlands of South Dakota, Wyoming, Utah, and Nevada, heading west down Interstate 80. I am now in my sixties and still go back and forth down Interstate 80, visiting friends of family.

- 16 -
FINDING MY FIRST BIBLE

When we got back to California, I stayed with my grandparents on my mom's side. I worked for my grandpa for a couple months.

Grandpa was Portuguese, and he was popular back in the day. He was hardworking and successful, and he had lots of business friends in San Leandro: the good old boys club. Grandpa grew up in Oakland, Hayward, and San Leandro in the California East Bay area. My grandma was Italian, from Chicago. Her mom moved from Chicago to California to get away from the fighting and murders of family members. Grandma's dad, my great-grandpa, was from Italy. He was a bootlegger for the Black Hand, Al Capone's gang. My great-grandma said Al Capone kissed her hand at a party one time.

I remember going to Great-Grandma's house for Sunday spaghetti feasts with all her kids and their kids, until Grandma passed away. We did that a few times with Mom and her mom and two kids. In Chicago, Great-Grandpa Sam had a couple restaurants in the early 1980s, and then he passed away. Sam was not his real name because back then, criminals would get into trouble and then change their names.

When I was living in South Dakota and my grandpa was still living in Chicago, I wanted to go see him. A friend of mine, Joey, grew up in Chicago and said he'd go with me, and so we headed out. I was in my early twenties and wanted to go see my great-grandpa. I called Grandma in California to get his address, and she yelled, "You stay away from them!"

Wow; she was right. Looking back now, I would have said to Grandpa Sam, "I want in the family business." I was a kid, looking for my place in life.

Grandpa told me as a kid in the California Bay Area, they would stand on the corner of Twenty-Third Avenue in Oakland and jingle change in their pockets. That's how Jingle Town got its name.

Grandpa was born in 1923 and was a hardworking man. I asked him how he got such big muscles. He told me rowing his rowboat across San Francisco Bay from Oakland. He would dismantle old wood boats and then sell the wood for firewood. Grandpa was in the Navy and built ships in World War II. In 1945, after the war, he went back to working in automotive repair shops. At one time, he had five or six auto repair shops in the East Bay. He also owned a brake factory in Hayward and an auto parts store in Oakland.

Grandpa worked double shifts to save the money to buy his shops. Back in the 1970s, he built a three-floor apartment building in San Leandro. The apartment building was his last, biggest project. In the 1980s, Grandpa and Grandma bought six acres in Danville, California, and built their dream house. After a few years, Grandma passed away from cancer, and about fifteen years later, Grandpa passed away too.

Around 1998, I told Grandpa I was going to write a book. He asked me, "What do you have to write about?" Grandpa was loud and not very nice at times, but I loved them both and respected them for being my family. The reason Grandpa said that was he did not know how I came to the Lord, because I lived out of state. By the time I understood enough to share it with them, they were gone. Jesus said "a prophet is not without honor except in his home town and among his own relatives and in his own household" (Mark 6:4 (NIV)). You have better results speaking to others in a farther away place, where you do not know anyone, and they can't use your past mistakes against you.

I needed a car. I was nineteen and ready to launch. Mom, Ted, and the rest of us just got back from Minnesota. I asked Grandpa if he had a job I could do. I needed to make some money to buy a car. He said he needed help cleaning out an apartment. An elderly woman had passed away, and her apartment needed to get cleaned out. I loaded the stuff into his truck for the dump. I was shocked because there was so much good stuff in there. I asked Grandpa why he was throwing this stuff out when some of it was good. He said the family came and took what they wanted, and so the rest is going to the dump. He did not save stuff like I did.

We loaded the truck with her stuff. While cleaning up, I found an old Bible and two old handmade dolls, a rabbit and a hillbilly named Snuffy. These were the only things I could sneak out. My grandpa did not want me to keep anything. I still have them today. I took that Bible with me from that day forward, state to state, year after year; it was always with me. I am kind of shocked that as much as I moved around, I did not lose the Bible and those two dolls. I did not know anything about religion or the Bible. I still thought Jesus was Santa Claus's baby. I believed there was a God, but that is about it.

I worked for Grandpa a couple months, saved some money, and bought a 1968 Chevy pickup truck with a 327 engine, step side, short bed. I had some wheels and did not have to rob anyone to get it. Thank God.

I was still talking to Gloria, the Native girl I met in South Dakota a couple months earlier. She wanted to come to the West Coast. She had never left her hometown before. I wanted her to come too; it was a big step for her. She took a flight and flew to California to visit me and see the West Coast. She liked it and stayed. We both got full-time jobs. I started working at a body paint shop, and the owner taught me how to fix dents. It was cool doing body work; it was a fun job. We had a hard time finding someone to rent to us because we were both so young. Apartment or house, we did not care. After a month of looking, we finally decided to pray and asked God to help us find our own place, and that day, we got an apartment. Before long, Gloria got pregnant. She had a baby girl already, who stayed with her mom in South Dakota when she came to the West Coast.

"Boat of Salvation"

This was the first time Gloria had been off the reservation. She was seventeen. We lived in California about a year, but when she got pregnant, she wanted to go back home to South Dakota. Some of my family did not make Gloria feel very welcome, and that did not help her to want to stay.

- 17 -
BACK TO SOUTH DAKOTA

We loaded up the Chevy truck and moved to South Dakota, taking Interstate 80, east out of Reno, across Nevada, Utah, Wyoming, and then north over the Black Hills of South Dakota across the Badlands. Twelve miles from the Minnesota border and near the North Dakota border, we stopped in Sisseton. This was the same small town Ted took me hunting a couple years earlier, where I met Gloria. Living on the reservation was different from just hunting for two days and going to a party. I found out real fast it was not like where I was from.

After living with the Native people, hearing their stories of the past, I have lots of respect and love for them. I had no idea about the history of Native Americans or the suffering they endured. I watched TV in the 1960s and 1970s, where Indians were made out to be savages, the bad guys. I never really thought about the history of America. I was raised in California, and nobody ever said much about your race or color. I mean, history never was a subject while growing up. I remember seeing *The Last of the Mohicans* in school; I thought it was the last Indian alive. When I went hunting with Ted and went to the Native American center back in Minnesota, I learned the Indians were still alive.

Living on the reservation with Gloria was very enlightening; I learned about their modern-day culture and their mistreatments of the past from settlers taking their land and killing them; they almost wiped them out. Really? They didn't surrender? Funny, I knew way back then; I would talk about the Native people to other people. I did not know I would be writing a book about God, and this is a good opportunity to write about living with the Native Americans. I knew someday I would tell my story about living on a reservation and talk about the pain and death Natives were subjected to by people coming here. It was a bad deal. I do believe America has become a beacon of light and freedom to the world now, and what started out with death to Native people ended up a good thing in different ways. Had Russia or China or the Muslims taken the land, they may have wiped the Natives off the earth.

I needed to get a job. I looked around and ended up working for a guy named

Dave, who had a mechanic shop in Sisseton. He also did body and paint work in his shop, and I helped out doing body work stuff. The first or second day in Dave's shop, I saw an old Harley Davidson hanging up in the rafters, in the corner of the shop. The corner was kind of dark, and the bike was black, so I could not see it very well, but I felt like that old bike was saying "Save me." This was no ordinary Harley hanging in the rafters.

I asked Dave, "What's the story on the bike?"

He said, "That's Billy's bike. He is in prison, and the bike is being stored here."

Not too long after starting at Dave's, I got into some trouble and spent two weeks in jail. My friend and I were drinking with a couple girls at a motel; we got kinda loud, so the police were called. They claimed my friend and I resisted arrest; one of the charges was aggravated assault on a police officer. My elbow broke the side back window in the cop car while they put us inside it. The cops tried to make a bigger deal out of it than it really was. So I got out on work release for two weeks. It wasn't too bad.

Ten years later, I found out why the cops really arrested me. A Native friend of mine, Rick, was a Sisseton police officer, and I asked him about that arrest. He told me the owner of a chicken restaurant in Browns Valley, Minnesota, called and wanted me arrested. The owner told his friend, a police officer, to arrest me for something, anything, and he would get a free dinner. Why? Because Gloria and I went to dinner there one night, and I ordered shrimp; when I ordered, I asked the waitress if the shrimp was real or breaded.

She said it was real, so I ordered it, but it turned out to be breaded, ground-up shrimp. It was not real, so I sent it back and ordered something else. The owner came to our table and asked for my name and said, "What am I supposed to do with the shrimp now?"

I said, "Whatever you want. I asked the girl if it was real or breaded, and she said it was real."

It was not; that's how that happened. God, help me please, that was the first time I felt like I got railroaded in Sisseton for nothing.

Not too long after this happened, I quit working for Dave. In those days, I never stayed at one place for very long. Gloria and I moved to Minneapolis; she got pregnant, and our first baby, Julie, was born in 1979. I worked jobs at day labor, off and on.

One day, I found out about you could make twenty dollars donating blood down at the blood bank. My first visit, I got in line, and they gave me a blood donor number. I didn't notice the number, and when I went back the second time, a year or so later, they asked me what my donor number was. I couldn't remember, so they looked it up by my name and told me it was 1945. Suddenly, I was aware of this number like never before. I thought I was feeling something inside me, moving and speaking to my insides. I knew I was experiencing something. I knew this number meant something. I just did not know what or why.

We left Minnesota and went back to South Dakota again and headed to California, to the Bay Area. When I can see Mt. Diablo, I feel like I am home. We had another kid, Brenda, and we looked for a happy place to raise our family. For about a year or so, we worked in California and had a nice apartment in the foothills in East San Leandro.

I was trying to be a good dad and boyfriend, but something was missing. I think we just could not find that place that makes us both feel happy and peaceful at the same time. Gloria seemed to be wanting to be back on the rez again in South Dakota. Time to move. Our relationship was not getting better at this point, and she must have felt the same way.

I still have that old Bible I got while working for Grandpa in 1978, to this day. I didn't read it back then because I didn't understand it. I tried, but it was too hard to read, and back then, I thought it was just a book some guy wrote about God.

Gloria and I just raised our kids and, you know, just lived life in general; we did a lot of drinking and smoking pot, and I got in some average bar fights.

We moved back to Sisseton. One day a guy came to the house and asked if I could haul his bike to the agency village; it turned out to be Billy. So I did; I still wanted that bike badly. It was hanging up in Dave's repair shop a couple years earlier. It was the old 1945 Flathead Harley, with mostly original parts. While driving to the village, I asked Billy if he wanted to trade my truck for his bike. He laughed, and so I did not ask again. I dropped him and the bike off. I wanted that bike. A couple years went by, and I saw Billy somewhere and asked him if he remembered me asking to trade my truck for his bike.

He said, "You were kidding, right?"

I said, "No, I wanted that bike."

He said he sold it to this guy who was selling it again, so Gloria and I went down to the gas station where he worked and asked if he was selling the old Harley. Yes, he was. I didn't have the money to buy it that day, so I talked Gloria into buying it. She wanted it anyway. For the first couple years, she rode it, and I rode my bike. I checked the engine numbers on the engine case, and it was a 1945.

A couple years later, she sold it to me. I rode it a couple years and then sold it back to her, back and forth for about a twenty-year span. We both had our reasons for loving that bike. In a funny way, it was like holding on to our youth. Many old memories were attached to it. She still has the bike to this day. The memories of when we were in our twenties, into our thirties and forties, having kids, crossing the land; the bike was like part of the family.

- 18 -
DREAMS MEAN THINGS

It was now 1983, and we had another baby girl, Susan. I remember this like it was yesterday. In 1983, we parked the '45 Harley in the living room. We lived in the housing projects in Sisseton, and the house didn't have a garage. I remember wondering if my Bible's copyright date was 1945, because I got a receipt at the store while living in Minnesota a couple months earlier for $19.45.

I remember saying to Gloria, "There is that number 1945 again."

She just shrugged her shoulders. That number, I told her, was speaking to me somehow. Nobody ever knew what to say about my number thing. At that point, I did not know what it all meant, either. I just knew it was moving inside, speaking to me, telling me to save the things I was getting. I still have most of them today and am showing them in this book.

So I was thinking that the power of the Word of God, the Bible, was calling me. So I looked again in the Bible for the copyright date, and it was not there.

I still thought Jesus was Santa Claus's baby. I had been lied to so much in my life and ripped off enough; I did not want to fall for a Jesus Christmas baby story, so I stayed away from that truth for years, much too long.

I knew I was getting closer to my discovery of God. It was like the Lord was reaching out to me with this number somehow, for some reason. After a while, I did tell other people what I was going through because nobody understood it; most of them said things to discourage me.

I would pray and say, "Lord, if it is you, keep giving me signs and messages and dreams, things I could save to show my family and friends I am not crazy. So I know what I am seeing, feeling, hearing, and experiencing is really you, God. All right?"

Think about what I am really saying in my book; you don't hear stories like mine in today's world. Really, miracles by number? It would be astronomical that God would set things up for me from the past for the future, to find and leave evidence of Himself doing things for me in another realm of time and have a four-digit code to manifest itself. God and I would ride that wave inside me for years. It is easier if people just say it is nothing: "Stop it, Buster."

Things like this are laughed at in today's world. The Bible calls it unbelief. Many people don't believe in God, so why believe my story? I was not even going to write this book because I thought nobody would believe it. Yes, in the beginning, I had doubts myself. Would you keep saving things with a number on it for thirty years if you thought God asked you to? I believe it was God, so I did listen.

I have no idea why this particular number was used. I didn't wake up one day and think of a story that would take thirty years to put together, that's for sure.

The biggest miracle for me out of the whole deal was, I got saved. The final outcome is salvation for me, so it's a big deal for me: my biggest miracle of all. Sometimes, it's the outcome of events that is most important, not the little things that lead you to the discovery. Think about this for a minute: How many times has a number led you to giving your life to Christ Jesus? Never? And if this was me or the devil making this up for some reason, would we lead ourselves to Jesus and the reading of the Bible? Because I have had people say that maybe it's the devil doing this to me. I don't think Satan and his demons were too happy to see me get saved and covered by the blood of Jesus and learn about how to fight evil with the Word of God and help others find their way to the truth, do you?

Numbers can be a perfect order. That is why computers use numbers to build things and come up with perfect equations.

I went back to South Dakota again, on my motorcycle this time. I had that old Bible with me and tried to read it a couple times. It was like "Thee children of Israel, O Lord, defeated the enemies of God's people." It just didn't mean anything to me for years.

From 1981 to 1984, while in South Dakota and Minnesota, I had a series of dreams. These dreams took place in a neighborhood I did not recognize. In one dream, I was walking on the fence between the houses. In another dream, I was jumping from one rooftop to another, and I climbed trees in the backyards of houses in this neighborhood. In one dream, I was hiding in the attic of a house. I was around the same house a lot, in the same neighborhood. In one dream, I was looking in a window while a man and girl were sitting on a couch. The guy pointed at me because he could see me through the glass. I had to squint my eyes and use my hands up against the glass because of the reflection and the glare on the glass. I had these dreams for two years or so. I did not think much about them until later.

Gloria and I were not getting along very good, and when we did get into fights, it was very ugly, so I would leave town. I was on my way back to California. Any truck driver will tell you, going down those long highways, you can find parts of yourself inside you did not know were there.

```
                    1945
   1= means unity or commencement

   9= Finality of Judgement (3x3, the
   product of Divine Completeness)

   4= Creative works 3 + 1

   5= Divine Grace

   1945= 389 x "5"

      "3" Significant of Divine perfection
   and Completeness: resurrection, "new-
   ness of life"

      "8" Resurrection, regeneration,
   CONVERSION (a process). The eighth is a
   "new first."

   "9" Finality of Judgment. (See above)

   3 + 8 + 9 = 20

   "20"= "two tens"  "

      "2" TWO = Difference (either harmony
   in agreement toward conclusiveness, OR
   opposition, enmity, and division. A
   Conflict number: decisions of life and
   death.)

      "10" ten = Ordinal perfection.
   Another new first.
```

"Number Values"

I had lots of talks with God on the long stretches in those Midwest states, on motorcycles, cars, trucks, hitchhiking, free as a bird. One time, I was on my motorcycle in South Dakota; it was wet and cold, and I was heading back to California, so I bought a 1962 four-door Oldsmobile Dynamic 88, for a hundred dollars. I changed the oil, tuned it up, bought new tires, and took out the back seat out; then I took the front forks and tire off the bike and put it in the back. It drove fine all the way back to the West Coast. I took the '62 Olds to a flea market in Hayward and sold the car in ten minutes for seven hundred dollars. It was a nice car, and I wish I still had it.

My brother Joe and his wife, Julie, were renting her grandma's house in Pittsburg, California. I knew where Pittsburg was, but I had not been to their house yet. Pittsburg was next to Concord, my old stomping grounds. I knew Julie very well. We went to junior high school together and lived on the same street in Clayton. She is a beautiful person and was one of my best friends. I can see why Joe married her.

It was 1985, and we did not have cell phones back then, so I called my mom from a phone booth and got their address. As I drove through their neighborhood, the closer I got to the house, the more I felt this was the neighborhood I had dreamed about a couple years earlier. When I got to their house, it didn't look like the house in my dreams, but driving through the neighborhood gave me goosebumps.

Julie was home, and we visited for a while. She began to tell me what I had missed the past two years while I was away and got very upset. My brother was going crazy.

She told me he was seeing things, and it was the same things I was dreaming about. She called the police because she was scared and did not know what else to do.

He was doing methamphetamine a lot, and a couple times, they had to take him out of the house in a strait jacket. He was locked up for a while in a psychiatric ward. I was shocked and worried; I wondered if my dreams could have been part of Joe's hallucinations. Were my dreams somehow connected to his experiences? I know dreams can warn us, help us, and scare us, but I did not know how my dreams could be connected to what Joe was seeing.

Julie said Joe saw someone jump from their roof to the neighbor's roof one night. I had that dream. He said someone was in the attic of their house. I had a dream I was in the attic of a house. Joe said people were climbing in the trees in the back yard. I had that dream too. He said someone was walking on the fences. I had that dream. He said he saw someone looking in their window at them while they were doing a line of methamphetamine on their coffee table. I had a dream I was looking in a window at a girl and guy.

Joe told Julie, "See! Look, can you see someone was looking in our window, watching us."

I do not know if Julie remembers all this, but I do. I remember her telling me he was taken to the hospital's psych ward. I also had dreams of being in the psych ward of a hospital. I talked to Joe later about all this, and he didn't know what it all meant, either. I think I understand it better now because of my learning process, my experiences, and the wisdom I gained after sixty years and with the help of the Spirit of God.

Joe told me about some of the things that were bothering him. He was seeing spirits and hearing voices. He also was using drugs; yes, I am no angel: I used different kinds of drugs too, just not as much as he did. Joe said he knew someone who was into devil worship, and he was at the guy's house one night, watching them chant. He went over there to pick something up, not to participate in the devil worship. He said after that, he could never get the chants out of his mind, and it led to more evil things working inside of him.

That combination was enough to put Joe over the edge, and on March 4, 1985, he committed suicide. I'll never forget that day because I was working in Pleasanton. Joe came home from work early that Monday, and while I was at work, gazing out a window, I heard an explosion in my mind. It was not like a sound I heard before; it was loud enough to get me to wonder what it was. I thought someone just died in some other part of the world, then I felt hungry, lonely, and thirsty, all at the same time. I drove up to the store only two blocks away and sat there, thinking that I missed my kids, then I turned around and went back to work.

About twenty minutes after I heard the blast, my boss came out to the shop to say my mom was on the phone for me. She told me Joe just shot himself; he was in the hospital in Pittsburg. My heart sunk. I am sure now that was the explosion I heard: the gunshot. How I heard it was a mystery (Pittsburg is about forty-five miles away from Pleasanton).

I think my brother and I had a connection, much like twins, a spiritual connection that cannot be seen with the eyes. A couple weeks before he left us, I asked Joe if Dad ever picked him up from jail late at night, and he had no shoes on.

He said, "Yes, how did you know that?"

I said I had a dream. Dad asked me where my shoes were. And the night he picked him up from jail, Dad asked Joe, "Where are your shoes?"

"King Jesus"

One night, Joe told me about the evil that seemed to be hunting him down.

I asked, "What do you mean?"

He said the voices kept telling him to do things he didn't want to do.

"Like what?" I asked him.

He said, "Like running my car into a brick wall." He had a 1968 Camaro at that time. He said the voice told him he would kill his upcoming baby (Julie was about six months' pregnant at this time). I think he just did not want to live anymore. Fighting the drug habit and the evil that was pressuring him was just too much.

Do I understand this all? No, I do not. I just know it is real. Joe sat on the couch in the house they rented from Julie's grandparents and shot himself with a shotgun. Julie came home from work and found him. It was not easy going back there. I went back to the house to stay with Julie for a couple weeks. I started spending more time with Julie, along with other friends from the neighborhood and from school.

Julie and Joe always had lots of people coming to their house to party. I realized how bad the meth, cocaine, crack, and dope problem was. I had been living out of state and did not see dope like this until I got back to the West Coast. Most of my friends were high on meth for days. I learned what a tweaker was fast. My brother was out of control, staying up for six days at a time without sleep, becoming like a walking zombie.

- 19 -
MY LETTER FROM GOD, 1945

While I stayed at Julie's after Joe died, I decided to save some things to honor my brother's memory. I looked around the garage and found an old handmade doll. It was my old doll. Joe must have taken from one of my boxes of stuff I kept at our grandpa's barn in Danville. I had two dolls, the same age, probably made as a pair. Not long after that, I learned my mom had the other doll, a rabbit. So Mom got one of my dolls, and Joe had the other one. They both went through my boxes while I was gone; kind of funny, now that I look back. I got those two old dolls the same time and place I found my first old Bible, while cleaning out the apartment in San Leandro for Grandpa when I was nineteen. Nobody stole the Bible from me, right? I had the Bible with me all the time.

I looked through Joe's garage for some other things and put his straw cowboy hat away. Julie didn't seem to want me to take his stuff. If I asked for something, she would say, "I am saving that for the kids." So I had to sneak stuff out of the house.

After looking in the garage for a while, I opened a box and came across an old blue envelope. It said "Frank's first hair cut by Uncle Buster" with a line pointing to 1945. At that moment, I heard the voice of God, like I always did when I saw that number. It is hard to describe, but the voice said to me, "I knew your name in 1945 before you were born. I am God and can do anything. Nothing is beyond my ability to do." God told me to save the envelope, which had been prepared for me in 1945, fourteen years before I was born.

I asked Julie about it, and she said it was her Uncle Frank's hair in the envelope. It was her grandma's stuff in the box, and of course, the hair was for memories in their time, forgotten about until God gave it life again and spoke to me. I felt goosebumps, which made it even more real. The picture shows the blue envelope, along with the receipt I got in Minnesota. God gave me this envelope to add to my story and show me He knew my name before I was born.

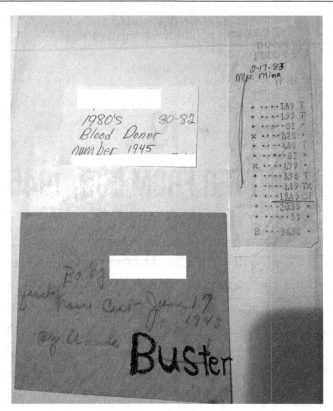

"Envelope from God"

God knew I would be born a few years later. This book's publisher suggested I not use my real name for legal reasons, so I am using "Buster," but God knew my real name. I used Buster for my story, and God would use this number 1945 to speak to me, to draw me to Himself for His plan of my surrender. The Father is awesome. He is all knowing, full of mercy, love, and grace, leading me to my salvation. Is this asking too much to believe? I mean, if anyone could do this, it would be God, right?

At this point, I know it may seem like my imagination or wishful thinking, but it was real and life changing. The first couple years I noticed this pattern of numbers and the experiences of voices, inspirations, and feelings, it was real to me, that's for sure. I wouldn't save a receipt from the grocery store for thirty years for no good reason.

This envelope was lost in time, if you think about it, sitting in a box nobody had any use for anymore, but God did. It would be in the garbage if I had not saved it. I gave the hair back to Julie's mom. She must have thought I was crazy, but I'm used to that.

Most of God's people in the Bible were killed or cast out away from others because people did not understand why God does what He does and chooses His people to tell the world about Him. So rather than accept the truth of God's power or the prophets or people in His church, they kill His chosen people to stop the Word of God's truths. Ungodly people do not believe.

Hearing that still soft voice speak in those moments helped my relationship with

Him grow. The voice of God would say, "Save this number for later with the other things," so I would. Saving anything was like a miracle in itself. I moved around a lot, and family members dug into my boxes of stuff.

It's not just the number; it is the message after seeing the number flowing through me. The discovery in the moment was moving me closer, drawing me to the truth of God; that was what He was doing. God really does work in mysterious ways, making sure I found that envelope. Putting it in my path proved to me God can do anything; even the smallest things can have a purpose in a big way in a person's life. If you think about it for a minute, you can see the beauty in receiving the envelope that was created with my name on it before I was born. In the book of Jeremiah, God says He knew your name before the foundations of the world. It took me years to find later in time, but I can appreciate the wonder that He created this for me, moving me closer and closer to His plan.

Years before I found this envelope, the Lord told me the number 1945 would be one of my signs from Him; He said in time, I would understand what it means to save what He gives me, like pieces of a puzzle telling a story. I was not thinking a story for a book, but I was obedient to what was asked of me, so I kept saving the things He said to save. Even before I wrote this book, I told my testimony to people, and it helped them. I found the people who believed my testimony would come to have a relationship with Jesus. This testimony will live on into the future because God's truths and His children never die.

- 20 -
VOICE CALLING MY NAME

About a month after Joe passed away, I was at work; I was the only one there, working on a car in the garage, and I heard someone whisper, "Buster!" I turned and looked but did not see anyone. Then I thought maybe I did not hear anything. Then a couple seconds later, someone called, "Buster," like a whisper again, but loud enough to hear for sure this time. I walked over to the wall to look around the corner; I thought someone was messing with me at first, then I realized nobody was there.

By then, I had gone down the walkway to see if anyone was there. I went down to where we clean up the cars; there was a pile of a couple hundred coins, mostly pennies. It was a big pile. As I turned to head back to work, a voice in my head said to look at the pile of pennies.

I was like, okay.

The voice said, "Without looking, reach into the pile and pull out a 1945 penny."

So I reached into the pile, ran my fingers around a bit, and then pulled out, yes, a 1945 penny. I thought it was like magic. At that moment, I heard that voice say, "With God, all things are possible."

I was like, wow. That was cool. I looked up and asked God, "Is that you?" But I did not hear an answer.

I could not stop thinking about it. I wondered where I should put the penny; I wanted to save it and not mix it with my other change, or lose it, or forget and spend it. So I put it on the floor of my truck until after work. I would put it in a better place, with my other 1945 pennies at home. At this point, I had a few 1945 pennies in my collection. I was finding them all over.

About an hour later, my girlfriend came to the shop and asked to use my truck. I gave her the keys, but after she left, I thought, *Oh no, she had her son with her, and he is going to take my penny.* I just knew it. She brought my truck back and gave me the keys. When I got off work, I went to my truck and looked down; yes, my penny was not there. Sad face.

After I got home, I called her and asked if her son had taken a penny from the floor of my truck. She asked her son, and he said he did not have it. I told her the penny meant a lot to me. It was a 1945 penny. I did not explain why it was so important or what it meant. She called me back to say she got it from him. Happy face.

I really wanted that penny back. It meant all things were possible with God. I still have that penny today, although it was hard getting it back from that evil little boy (just kidding; smiley face).

Looking back now, I know I never would have pulled that penny out of the pile had I not followed the voice I heard calling my name. I was prepped for that event by God. I am not a magician, nor do I have any power like that by myself.

- 21 -
PREMONITION OF THE RAPE

Turning the page to other strange things, I have a newspaper clipping to prove a premonition I had one night. The news clipping is about a man who kidnapped and raped a fourteen-year-old girl in Dublin, California. I will never forget this.

In 1986, I was visiting my mom for a couple months and worked at an auto body shop in Dublin. One evening, my mom's neighbor, Jennifer, invited me over to visit and smoke some weed. They just moved in a couple days earlier, so I went over and met her and her kids. She had two little boys and two girls, about eleven and fourteen. The neighbor also had two friends at the house that night while I was there, Steve and Brenda; they were a little older than me.

I'll never forget this: I said goodbye and left; as I walked out the door, I had the strangest thought. I thought to myself, *You should kill Steve. He's going to do something very bad to this family.* That bugged me. I never had a thought like this before, and to this day, I've never had a thought like that again. But all night, I kept thinking about this thought I had about Steve.

So the next morning, I was getting in my car to go to work; Jennifer was outside with her daughter and her daughter's boyfriend.

I walked over and asked her who Steve was. She said he was their friend and she'd known him for about ten years. She asked me why I asked, but I did not tell her what I thought about him. However, I told her I thought he was going to do something bad to them. I did not know what it was, just a feeling, I said.

Jennifer said, "It's all good," and left.

I went to work, and I felt better because at least I had warned them. Unfortunately, a couple hours later, while Jennifer was at work and the kids were home, Steve went over and kidnapped the fourteen-year-old girl.

He asked her to show him where the store was. When I asked her what happened a couple days later, she said she wanted to get him out of the house, away from the rest of the kids, so she went with him. He knew where the store was; he just wanted to get her away from the house. Then he asked her to run away with him.

She said she kept saying no, she did not want to run away with him. He showed her a large amount of cocaine he had. After she said no again, he pulled his gun out and pointed it at her, and they drove away. He raped her a couple times through the day and then dropped her off in another city. Now that is evil.

If I asked Jennifer today if she recalls me warning them that morning before Steve kidnapped her daughter, she'd probably say she did not remember. Too much time has passed by, and people do not always remember, but I do.

My sister says she remembers a police car in our garage in Hayward. She was around four years old. Twenty years later, she said she remembered I stole the police car. Right. Okay, here is what happened: A cop car was parked in front of our house, for some reason, and I stole the cherry off the roof of the car. I made a lamp shade out of it for a couple days. The police thought it was me and called my mom and asked for it back, so we gave it back.

I have documents to prove most of my stories. That always helps.

I always try to document my experiences for my testimony, knowing it is all important.

I am leaving out lots of smaller experiences, but a person can only remember so much, right? Like dreams. It is strange; at times, you know you had a dream, but you cannot remember it if your life depended on it. It's blocked, for some reason. Then you are walking down the street or driving down the road or talking to someone five years later, and that dream pops into your mind. I think this happens for a deeper reason. I have had lots of them, too many to mention.

- 22 -
HEADING TO BILLINGS, MONTANA

A couple years after Joe died, my grandmother passed away. After she passed, Grandpa was throwing stuff away, and I felt a tug on my spirit to see what he was throwing away. I waited till he walked away from the garbage and saw a letter my grandpa wrote to my grandma when he was in the Navy. It was dated 1945, so I grabbed it to add to my collection. After reading it, I almost cried, it was so cute. The letters said the boys really look forward to getting mail and pictures, and asked Grandma to take some pictures of herself with my mom and Grandpa's mom and send mail. Grandpa said he would write two letters a day to Grandma. He told her how much he loves and misses her, and he can't wait to come back home when the war is over.

"1945 Coins"

This picture shows some of the 1945 coins I have found. A couple of them were given to me by my kids and friends that I told my story to through the years.

At this point in my life, I knew God was communicating with me, telling me Who He was. I just did not know Who God really was yet; I still thought the Bible was just a book some guy wrote about God. I did believe the book was true, for some reason, not sure why. In my mind, Jesus was a fairy tale. I did not really know that Jesus was in the Bible up to that point in my life. What I am trying to say is, I did not think Jesus was a real person, but I believed God was real.

This is how I look at my state of mind back then: Like a Jew, I believed in God, just not Jesus. Most Jewish people believe in the God of Israel, but not Jesus. A person with half of the truth of the Lord's salvation plan is not complete. After you receive Christ as your Lord God, then you receive God's salvation plan in full, becoming a spiritually completed person. Completed spiritually by faith, not by works, lest any person boast (Ephesians 2:8-9 (NIV)). Having faith in the finished work of Jesus on the Cross, by faith we are saved, not by anything we can do.

Sadly, even though I knew I was building a relationship with God, I was still lost in my sins: a liar, thief, selfish sinner, destined for a dark, sad life, condemned without Christ, the Creator God of all things in heaven and on earth. One day, a friend and I were shopping at the Salvation Army, and I told him about my number thing; I picked up at a book and told my friend that it would have 1945 in it. It was a flight recorder book. I tore out a page and saved it, but because of confidential rights, I cannot share it here. It was not like a miracle, but I did add it to my stuff.

I wish I could remember all the awesome answered prayers and things God has done for me, but there are just too many to mention. He sends angels to help protect and guide us in our lives. We get benefits like that, blessings from the heavenly Father while we are alive. This is another one of God's promises. And there is proof He keeps His promises, every one of them. Out of thousands of promises the prophets wrote down in scripture, almost all have come to pass: proof of His Word being true. Humanity is down to only a few more promises and prophecies left to come true from the Bible, and Jesus will be back to get His church and finish this battle with evil. He already defeated death on the cross, more proof this is not a silly man-made game.

Gloria and I were still talking on the phone. Christmas was coming soon, and the timing was right to get out of Dodge again. By this time, Gloria moved from South Dakota and was going to a college in Billings, Montana. I just purchased a 1976 Trans Am that needed some rust repairs and paint work, but it ran well. I bought it from Henry, a friend in Pittsburg, but I did not know that the car was used to smuggle drugs.

I was already being watched by DEA before I even left to Billings. Anyway, I snorted up my last bag of meth. By this time, I was using the stuff too much. I told myself, "Buster, this is your last bag of go-fast," and hit the road to go visit my kids in Montana. I got to Billings late at night, went into the house and slept a little, and woke up to give hugs and kisses to the kids before they went to school.

I had been in Billings for just a few hours; I walked out to my car to bring in my stuff, and as I grabbed my bags, a guy walked over and asked me if I wanted to burn a joint. I thought, *Cool, yes, that would be nice.* Before we finished smoking, he asked me if I wanted to do a line of meth (seriously, this stuff is everywhere in this world). Yes, I will take a line, thank you.

I told the guy I just left California to get away from drugs and visit my kids, so don't bring dope around me after this. I never saw that guy again, but I did encounter others who were doing it. I was trying to stop using dope, but Gloria also was using, and so we did it from time to time while I lived in Billings.

Gloria told me about her friend Kathy from Sisseton, who passed away not too long ago. Her husband Ben came home late one night, and she was in bed with another guy, and Ben beat them both with a bat. The guy got away, but Kathy suffered head injuries and was left to die. By the time someone found her the next day, she was dead.

Ben went to prison for about seven years. I remember seeing him after he got out; he said, "What's up, Buster?"

I said, "Hey, what's up?"

About a week after he got out of prison, Ben was in a bar and got in a fight; he killed the other guy, but the courts ruled it self-defense.

I did auto body work. It was always easy to find work in that trade. I worked for a couple different shops and also worked for myself. I started building a reputation around town as a good worker.

I met a godly man; for the first time, I had a friend who seemed to know things about God, and I believed him. His name was Roy. Nice guy. I worked a few days for him, stacking and moving tires. He bought and sold tires out of his house. I think he only befriended me to get me to his church, a Pentecostal church.

Not long after we met, he asked me if I wanted to have breakfast with some of his friends from church. They read verses out of the Bible before going to work. I said yes. Roy said to bring my Bible, if I had one. I still had that old Bible I found at Grandpa's years ago. I went to the restaurant and brought my Bible for the first time to read it with people who could help me understand it. Roy and three other guys were sitting at a table; one named Joe was sitting across from me and said, "That's an old Bible you got there. How old is it?"

I said I didn't know because I couldn't find the copyright date in it. Believe me, I had looked, thinking about my number 1945, but never found the date. Joe asked to see it and turned right to the date.

I said, "What?"

Joe said it was 1945. At that moment, like before, a voice spoke to my inner self, reminding me that He is God. I recalled the time I pulled the penny out the pile; I looked up and asked God if He did this. I knew I could not do magic, so God or His messenger said, "Yes, it was." God helped me pull that penny out of the pile without looking. All things are possible with God. He said He wanted me to read the Bible. This was what He was asking me to do: read my Bible. That was it. Wow, read my Bible; cool.

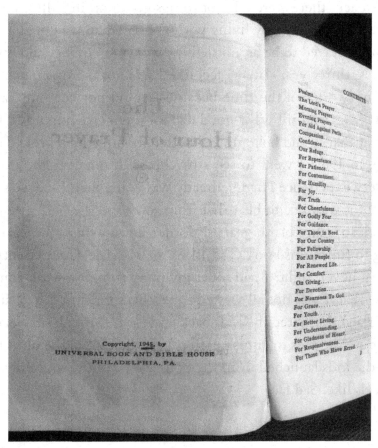

"1945 Bible"

Well, I was right; my Bible was marked with 1945. Funny how Joe turned right to it, but I couldn't find it. Trust me, I looked and asked other people to find the date. No one else found it.

Not long after discovering my Bible was from 1945, I got baptized at Roy's church, the Pentecostal church. It only took two Sundays after getting baptized before things started going wrong at home again. Gloria's sister, Leanna, was killed in a car wreck.

Gloria and Julie, our oldest daughter, left to go back to the reservation for the funeral. I watched our other two girls. I was okay with it, but after the first week, my boss stopped paying me. It was hard to feed and take care of the kids because I was broke. The next Sunday, I went back to church and told Roy that after getting baptized, my world was falling apart.

Roy said, "Buster, God is testing you."

I thought, *Really?* It reminded me of school, and I did not do well on tests there, either. I walked away from the church that day. Being tested by God, I felt like a fish out of water. I only knew how to break the law and be bad. I did not want to be tested by God. I did not understand the Bible yet; Jesus was still like Santa Claus's adopted child in the Christmas story. I was twenty-seven years old at this time.

As I think back, there were a lot of things going on in Billings. Our little family was three girls now. I did enjoy living with Gloria when we got along. I could be the nice daddy like I prayed to be as a little boy, working, loving, and providing.

The truth is, thirty years later, I feel like I was not there as much as I should have been. I was angry a lot of the time because I could not keep my family together. I asked my kids years later if I was a good dad for them growing up. They said I was, so I will leave it at that. It did help me feel better about being a good dad.

One time, in 1987, I went to see a psychic in Montana. The psychic told me to document every experience I had. I already was doing that. I started saving things and documents, but it was nice to hear that from someone else.

There were so many blank years; I do not know where the years all went. I am finally trying to finish this book God asked me to write about twenty-five years ago; better late than never, right? I had to let my pony run for a while longer, I guess.

I do know that it was not all wasted time, that's for sure. I had fun taking care of our kids. Gloria and I shared the kids back and forth through the years, but we didn't play games or use the kids to punish each other when we broke up. That was good for all of us. All the kids launched from the house successfully, and now I know what an empty nest feels like. Sad face.

- 23 -
STRANGE THINGS HAPPEN

Gloria and I had a couple friends in Billings we would go on rides with, smoke weed, drink; your average stuff. We broke up a couple times while I was there, and we dated other people. One day, Gloria came home from work and was crying, and I asked what happened. She said her boyfriend got into a wreck and died. On the one hand, I felt bad for her; on the other hand, I was not sad at all.

Here is the part of this sad story that is unusual: I was dating one of her friends from work, but she did not know about it. Both of us were seeing other people, still living in the same house, but living different lives half the time. I did not like it, but that was how it was. I was dating a girl I really liked and probably would have married her because back in those days, I did not make the best of choices. A couple months after Gloria's boyfriend died, the girl I was seeing also died in a car crash.

I had a friend, named Rick, who rides a Harley too. We would go for rides. Slick Rick was among my best friends, a real cool dude. He was the first guy who called me "45Buster" (because our Harley was a 45 flathead). I liked it.

Gloria, the kids, and I went back to South Dakota to visit family, and while we were there, I bought a truck from Gloria's mom. It was a 1968 GMC and had a nice, straight body, but the engine was tired, and I planned to replace it after we got back to Billings.

On our way back to Billings, Gloria was out in front of me. She was supposed to stay close because I didn't know if the truck would make it back to Billings; it was about a seven-hour drive in those days. I got pulled over for speeding by the highway patrol.

Well, the officer said I was high risk of skipping out of court and not paying the ticket, so I had to pay the fine on the spot or go to jail. That was a new one on me. I was broke because I used all my cash to buy the truck. Gloria was too far ahead, and back in those days, nobody had a cell phone.

The officer said he would call for me if I knew someone in Billings who could go down to the sheriff's office and pay the ticket in cash. The only person I could think of was my mom (LOL), but she was in California. I thought of another person who might do it for me: Ringo, a friend in Billings.

I was tight with Ringo, and we got along well. I did some paint work on one of his cars. The officer went to his car, made the call, and came back and said, "You owe Ringo eighty dollars."

He paid it, and they let me go. I told the officer to tell Ringo I had the money at home, and I could pay him the next day. The next day, guess who came to my house to visit? Yes, Ringo. I paid him back and thanked him. I remember how good it felt to have a friend who helped me out in a bad moment, where time and money were the biggest factors.

Not long after this, my boss asked me if I was a drug dealer.

I said, "Where did that come from, Steve?"

He said, "Your friend Ringo was a drug dealer, and you took two trips to California this past year."

I said, "Yes, to visit family. Steve, you've been to my house; we smoked weed together, and you know I don't have anything. If I was a dealer, don't you think I would at least have a nice car? And how do you know Ringo is a drug dealer?"

Steve said, "The DEA was in asking questions about you and Ringo. They said they were watching both of you for being in a drug ring from Mexico to California to Montana."

"Steve, I know Ringo has taken trips to Mexico from time to time, but I know nothing about him being a drug dealer."

About two weeks later, Ringo's wife came to my house and said he was in jail and wanted me to visit him. I went to the jail, but they would not let me see him. That was the last time I ever saw him.

One day, I saw a wrecked truck parked behind a farmhouse, so I walked over to the house, knocked on the door, and asked the people there if they would sell it. They said yes, and I paid them a couple hundred for it; I took the truck home, put the good front clip on it, and bingo, I had a cool 1968 GMC short-bed truck. Yes, the front part was red, and the back was light blue, but paint was all it needed to be nice. I did paint it not too long after that.

At the same time, I bought a Camaro from a used car dealer I did some work for. The funny part, not funny, but strange, was Rick came over soon after we had the truck and car parked out front.

He said, "Buster, you know that wrecked truck you got behind the barn?"

"Yes."

"I knew the guy who owned it."

And I said, "So?"

He said, "He's dead."

"Oh, sorry to hear that."

"But Buster?"

"Yes, Rick?"

"You know that Camaro your girl drives?"

"Yes, Rick?"

"I knew the owner of that Camaro too. The guy who owned that car killed the guy who owned your truck. He is in prison now for murder."

"Oh," I said. "That is strange."

He said, "Yes, it is."

At this point, I had been living in Billings around two years. That was usually the point at which I would leave. On my time off work, I built a camper for my truck because I knew I would be going back to California soon. Winter was coming, and it took a month to build this camper. A couple times while I was out back, working on the camper, I heard some gunshots.

"Owl"

We lived in town, so nobody should have been shooting a gun. One day, a woman walked down the alley behind the house while I was working on the camper; I assumed she was going to the store down the street. I said hi as she passed by. I was about done building the camper, and she stopped and talked to me. She said my camper looked nice, and I thanked her. I told her I probably would be sleeping in it soon. She said I should come over to meet her boyfriend. I said okay. I was heading to California soon, but I decided to meet her boyfriend first.

Gloria was not kicking me out, but we both knew I was leaving, like I always did when we had our fights or could not get along. So the next night, I ended up over at this lady's house, smoking weed, drinking beer, and talking to her boyfriend. They seemed like a cool couple. They must have been in their late thirties, early forties. He had a Harley parked out front. I stayed two nights.

The first night, after I had a couple beers, he asked me if I heard any gunshots lately. I said yes, I remembered hearing someone shooting a gun a couple times while I was outside working on my camper.

He said every time I heard a shot, he killed a guy.

I laughed at him and said, "Yeah, right, and you bury them out back?"

He said no, a cleanup crew came in, picked the bodies up, and took them somewhere else. He said wherever he went, he was protected by the federal government.

I looked this guy in the eye and could tell he was not kidding. He said he was involved in organized crime in Canada and turned state's evidence. The organization was worldwide, and he turned on them after finding out Russia was using them to build armies.

He said, "For my freedom and the preservation of America, I turned state's evidence, slowing down Russia's plans to destroy America from the inside. China and Islamic Jihadists are doing the same thing right now. They're getting more and more radicals voted into top offices in Washington."

This guy said the feds would make a sweep all around the world at the same time, busting the clubs for illegal weapons, drugs, large amounts of money, trying to stop the takeover of America. He added there was a contract out on his life.

I said, "Oh, is that all? Okay, I am okay with it."

I really didn't know what to say about it. He mentioned the names of some people in California I knew, so I figured he might be telling me the truth. After getting back to California, I asked my friends about this Russia thing going down. One friend knew about the hit on this guy from Canada but did not know about the Russia thing. Not too long after I got back from Billings, there was a large bust all around California and across the United States at the same time. Probably around the world as well.

- 24 -
BACK TO CALIFORNIA

I went back to California and wanted to stop at Julie's house, so I called over there, and her boyfriend Mike answered the phone. I told him I would be there around seven o'clock, but I got sidetracked until the next day.

When I went over to the house, Julie said, "Holy moly! It was a good thing you didn't come over yesterday."

I asked, "Why? What happened?"

She said cops dressed in all black, ninja style, raided the house around four o'clock and stayed there until ten at night. They thought a friend of mine, with the same name as me, was coming over and that is why they raided the house. He was one of my best friends from high school in Hayward. The DEA were looking for my friend, and when I called earlier that day, the phones were bugged, and they thought I was the other guy.

My friend was still a very active criminal at the time. He and I got busted doing an armed robbery when I was sixteen. We sold drugs, committed burglary, stole cars and motorcycles, committed assaults, and that was all before turning eighteen. I am not proud of my past, but I think it's important to show how bad I was so you can see how far God will go to bring you out of a dark place and restore you. He forgives us our sins when we ask.

The DEA wanted my friend bad, so it would seem. I think they thought I was a part of the drug ring too. But the truth is, I never was. I was just always in the wrong place at the wrong time, and my circle of friends were into bad stuff. I was a good boy (right).

I wanted to get back on track, in what God was doing with me, not what my sins were.

I went back to California two more times to visit before leaving Billings for good.

After two years in Billings and trying to be happy, I moved back to California and settled in a small town called Portola. Some friends were living up there. It was a railroad town forty miles west of Reno. I loved it up there. It reminded me of my grandpa's property. Grandpa moved a nine-bedroom house onto the property. Some of my best childhood memories were up there. We would go two times a year for fishing, hiking, swimming, and riding horses.

I lived in Portola for a couple of years. When I first moved up there, I lived with my friend for a couple of weeks and then got my own place. In 1988, I went down to the Bay Area to visit my mom, and Ted and I ended up bringing Ted's cousin, Larry, from Minnesota.

Larry was not his real name. I didn't know his real name because he was on the run for some crimes he committed in Minnesota. He stayed with me for a month or so, and it did not look like he would ever get a job, so I took him back down to my mom's and dropped him off.

Larry called back home to Minnesota and told the wrong people where he was, and the feds came knocking on my mom's door, looking for him. They soon found him in Dublin. Come to find out, Larry was on the TV show *America's Ten Most Wanted,* and someone in Minnesota got a ten thousand dollar reward.

I lived in Portola for a couple months, and then two of my daughters came and stayed with me for about a year. In 1989, Gloria came to Portola and lived with me for a couple months. She was pregnant at the time (not by me). She brought the old '45 flathead Harley, which she wanted me to buy again. Her baby was due soon, and she wanted to give birth in SD, so she left with our two girls, while I stayed in Portola.

There were always exciting things going on in Portola. One of my crazy friends, Fred, always added fun to the party. He was a hard worker and rode a Harley. I have nothing but respect for him because he is a bad boy from Jingle Town in Oakland, where my grandpa was from. Fred helped me realize life is too short to sit around. He would tell me to build something and not be lazy.

Fred said a lot of things; one thing I remember well, he told me, "Nice guys finish last."

I was working at a body shop down the road from Portola. After finding out Gloria wanted to sell me the bike, I had to scrape up some money. I had no furniture, so I went down the road looking for cabins that were closed but still had stuff in them. I got a bed, chairs, dressers, dishes all out of one cabin. I'm not proud of being a thief, but I was; sorry.

I left the dresser outside in the shed until the next morning. I needed to clean all the stuff out the drawers, so the next day, I was out there looking through the dresser, hoping to find something from 1945. I looked through every drawer, and there was nothing worth saving but some old football cards from 1952. I gave one of the cards to my buddy. I picked the dresser up to move it back into the shed, and as I set it down on the cement, a coin dropped out of it, making a sound as it hit the cement. I knew it was a coin.

I began to walk back to the house, but the ringing of the coin hitting the ground kept telling me it was a 1945 penny. At first, I kept walking away, but my thoughts told me to go see if I was right. I could not help it. I went back into the shed and moved the dresser out of the way, and, yes, it was a 1945 penny. I added it to my collection.

The message from God was to listen and never give up when looking for something because with Him, all things are possible, and you should not quit searching for what you believe in, especially if it is ringing in your ears.

Once again, I felt good about the importance of 1945 to me. Apparently, the penny was lodged underneath the dresser. It was not in the drawers where I looked. I dumped every drawer out, but somehow, after carrying the dresser down the hill, the penny got stuck somewhere inside.

A couple days later, my friend Kathy found a 1945 nickel at work. She worked in a small store in town and saved it for me. It is in my collection of 1945 coins. Most of my close friends have heard about my 1945 story for years. Nobody wanted updates on my number, so I stopped talking about it.

I liked Portola; it was an old railroad town in the mountains, where most people had bikes. There was always something going on, and Reno was only forty miles away.

Even though I had been baptized up in Montana, I was not seeking God out much. I did not want to go to church. Something was still wrong about Jesus; I didn't think He was real. I believed the Bible was true but had not yet discovered that Jesus was true too. I was a little confused about Who God was and how this number would help me, or why God was using the number.

Up to this point in my life, I had not read any of the Bible, even though God asked me to. I tried to read it, but it did not make any sense. So I stopped trying to read it.

One night, my daughter Julie woke up crying from a bad dream. She was kind of sleepwalking because she was awake, but the bad dream was still going on in her head. I got my Bible and started to read out of it, and her bad dream stopped. Years later, she and I talked about that bad dream; she still remembered how reading the Bible made the evil dream go away.

Next, I moved back down to Dublin, into my mom's house. I planned to work, save some money, and then go to SD again and try to be a family. In short, Gloria and I could not find our happiness but kept thinking it would show up for our kids' sake. Year after year, however, it was the same thing: good for a while, then it got dysfunctional. Then, repeat the cycle: moving from state to state, never finding our happiness.

I needed some new wheels, so I sold the 68 GMC and the Trans Am, and bought a 1960 Ford pickup. I painted it red, tuned it up, changed the oil, and headed back to the reservation in SD. Gloria and I had been broken up for almost two years this time, and she had another beautiful baby girl. At first, I was just going back to see my kids. I thought because she had a baby from someone else, I would not want to work it out with her anymore, but after staying with her for a couple days, I realized that I loved her new baby, named Kay, and wanted to be her dad.

Gloria and I normally stayed together two or three years every time we got back together. I stayed long enough this time to get her pregnant again with our son, the last one, Buster Jr. We finally had our boy. She had her tubes tied after five kids. We were living in Watertown, South Dakota, when we had our son. I was working at a couple different shops around town. Things were okay until a guy at work was fooling around and accidently hit me with a car and messed up my back. I was on disability for a year.

- 25 -
A BOY'S PRAYER ANSWERED

I am not proud of this next story I'm about to tell, but I think it's worth sharing how a boy's prayers were answered by God, through me.

It all started because ever since I was a young boy, I always wanted a lever-action .22. I've had a lot of rifles but never one as cool as I the one I saw in the back window of this pickup, parked close to our house. It was late 1992 in Watertown, SD. I waited till the sun went down and told myself if this guy left the gun in his truck and the windows were down, I was taking it. So after the sun went down, I went around the block, and yup, it was there, so I grabbed it and took it home. I put it in the garage until the end of summer; all winter it was covered up, and I forgot about it.

Later that spring, Gloria and I were not getting along (imagine that). One sunny afternoon, I was in Sisseton, about fifty miles north of Watertown, visiting family. I stopped at a friend's house, and we were looking for something to do. He said there was a street dance in this little town in Minnesota. It was about seventy miles away in Minnesota, so I headed down Interstate 29 South and started thinking that I should just sell that rifle I took. Rather than take a chance of going to jail for a hot gun, I thought it would be safer to sell in another town.

I pulled into this town I had never been in and drove down the main street; it didn't look like a street dance was going on, so I turned left and found a place to make a U-turn; some people called out to me to come over to where they were parked. They were drinking beer, and when I pulled over next to them, they asked me if I wanted to drink a beer with them.

Cool, okay, I cracked a beer open and told them I was looking for a street dance in town. They said there wasn't one. I decided to ask if they wanted to buy a .22 rifle, saying I hated to sell it but needed the money.

There were two guys and two girls there, and one of the guys said yes, he was looking for a .22. I said it's in Watertown if he wanted to follow me there. I had him park around the corner from my house and came back with the .22. The guy held the gun in his hands and came unglued. He was yelling and laughing, jumping up and down, and thanking Jesus.

He said he prayed night after night to get this gun back, explaining that his dad gave it to him when he was a kid; it was his first .22. He gave me the money, thanked me, and asked where I got it. I told him I bought it from someone at a bar a couple nights ago. God answered his prayers through my sin of it all, like a daddy brings his child back to the store to return what he wrongfully took. Aw, that was cute; I felt spanked. And the boy who prayed to God got his prayer answered. It was awesome how it all came down that day. I never told anyone about that because it's embarrassing. I stole a gun and then sold it back to the guy I took it from. Only the Lord gets the glory in this story. It was perfectly executed by Him. Amen.

- 26 -
A NAKED GIRL IS PASSED OUT IN MY BED

At this time, I was on disability for a year, and I was getting a one-time payment for my back injury from worker's comp. It wasn't much, and I didn't want to blow the money, so I found a forty-acre farm for twenty-thousand dollars. I put five thousand dollars down, and my mortgage was two hundred dollars a month. The house needed to be gutted and remodeled. The forty acres were fenced and close to Sioux tribal headquarters. My first winter there was hard, because I didn't have a plow to clear the snow on my private dirt road. Going in and out it was hard at times. One time, I could not get gas delivered for heat.

When I first bought the property, I was living with Gloria in Watertown, and of course things were not good between us around this time, so I ended up living on the farm by myself for one year. I bought a single-wide mobile home with two bedrooms and one bath from my boss, who gave me a good deal at fifteen hundred dollars. It was nice, and I liked it. I put in a septic tank and got electricity hooked up; it was all good for a while.

I called Bill, a friend of mine from California, to come out so we could grow some weed out there, but what did he do? He brought his little boy, and the boy's mama did not know he was going out of state. She called the police, and the sheriff chased Bill all the way back to California, which ended that plan.

One cold winter night, there was snow on the ground; I went to town for a beer and came home after closing time. There was a dirt road leading onto my property, about two hundred yards long to the house, off the main road. About halfway down my road, I saw a car was stuck. I got to my back door to go in and could see someone broke the door open. I went in and grabbed my pistol that I had hidden. A naked girl was passed out on my bed. I was in trouble.

I thought I was being set up or something. I was not sure what was going on. My bathroom mirror was broken, and they trashed my house. They drank all my beer and put all my CDs in a bag; just then, a kid came in the back door. He was drunk. I asked him what happened to my house. He said he did not know. I smacked him in the head with the butt of my gun, and then he remembered they got stuck on my road.

He said they broke into the house because they were cold.

I said, "Breaking in and drinking my beer was not so bad, but why did you guys trash my house?"

He said he did not know. It was his girlfriend who was passed out naked in my bed. I took him to the tribal police station because he was Native, and my land was in the middle of tribal land. I told the police officer about the girl passed out in my bed, and he followed me back to my house. The girl had put her clothes on but must have passed out again. He took her to police headquarters. About fifteen minutes later, I could hear the car that was stuck running, trying to get unstuck. I grabbed my gun, walked out to the car, and knocked on the window; when the person inside rolled down the window, I smacked them in the forehead.

It was another girl, who had been hiding, and she said, "Ouch!"

I said, "Oh, sorry, I thought you were a guy." It was dark out.

She came into the house, and I made her start cleaning up the mess they made. I told her, "Breaking into my house because it is cold and drinking my beer was not that bad, but trashing my house was wrong."

About fifteen minutes later, the tribal police came back to my house to get her. One of the other kids probably told them she was out there.

- 27 -
SMOKE SIGNALS FROM GOD

Not long after that, I started going out with Ronda. It was fun at first, and she helped me get over Gloria. We were together about two years. It was not easy finding a girl on the reservation. Gloria was, let's say, a rough mama after a few drinks, and none of the girls would go out with me because they were afraid of Gloria (or related to her). Ronda was another short ball of fire, and she was not afraid of Gloria.

Ronda was Native American, like most my friends. I had white farmer friends too. I will say whites out there were racist back then; they still treated Native people badly. It is better today, not much, but a little, I think.

Ronda had a friend named Chap. She introduced me to him and his wife. We would hang out with them, party, drink beer, smoke some doobies, and laughed until the sun came up; no fighting. I told Chap about my 1945 experiences and God. He was entertained.

I sold my forty acres, and Ronda and I moved to California. We came back to the reservation after a year. We saw Chap somewhere, and he said he had something for me at his house. We went over there, and he gave me a pack of chundies. Cigarettes. I told him I didn't smoke cigs, but he said, "Look at how old they are."

I looked on top, and it said 1945.

I said, "What? Where in the world could you find a pack of smokes from 1945?"

Chap said, "We were hunting last winter, and to get out of the cold, we went into an abandoned farmhouse and found a carton of smokes on a shelf."

They smoked them, looked to see how old they were, and yes, my number, 1945. Again, the Lord spoke to me saying, I am your friend. Chap said he thought of me because of the story I told him a couple years earlier. Cool. I added them to my collection of 1945 stuff.

"1945 Cigarettes"

Native people burn tobacco, sage, and other things for spiritual reasons or just for the fragrance and enjoyment of things the earth gives to us. The smoke can be sacred, supernatural. I try looking at all things in a spiritual way, on top of the normal way average people see things, in the flesh only. I think tobacco is a strong God-given medicine, a friendly messenger of the earth spirits. It was special for me to get a pack of smokes with 1945 on them from Chap, a good friend.

My heavenly Father knows how to reach me with a gift for my story. His power cannot be matched by humans. God speaks to me in this forever spoken Word. His words never die. After you read about what God is doing in me and around me, you'll start seeing the unbelievable things He can do.

MYSTERY SOLDIER
IN SEARCH OF THE TRUTH

"Cross of Christ"

Some people don't see the beauty of the different stories until later. Part of what works with God is surrendering to Him and believing He can do anything. Are you watching Him work on your behalf? Do you believe He is the Creator of all things? He can move what He wants when He wants, putting things in front of you to discover.

In endless time, He opens doors, and He closes doors in the physical realm, and in your mind's spiritual self, because He loves you, no matter what you've done in your life. There are no barriers that can keep the Father God out. I hope your inner door is open so the Lord can work on you and for you. Free will can be good, and it can be bad. Do you believe God would do something special for you to see a sign? He would, if you asked and are patient. God loves us so much He gave His Son as a living sacrifice.

God loves the little things in creation too. His miracles are not all big ones, like parting the Red Sea or letting it rain for forty days and nights or raising the dead. He brings nations up and brings nations down; giving sight to the blind; and the crippled walk again. We serve a God Who wants to show us He is real and not going away after one generation. The Lord has people all over the world speaking about the miracles He is doing for them. I know some of you readers are not saved by the blood of Christ, but I am praying you will be. The door to the ark of our salvation will close at some point, so enter in. Be walking with Jesus until the day He returns; be sure you are on board. The day of salvation is coming.

So getting back to my small miracle from Chap in South Dakota. To me, this gift was a holy smoke signal from God; it meant a lot. What comes from the earth goes back to the earth someday. It was extra shocking to find a pack of smoke signals dated 1945. I was excited to see God at work, behind the curtains of my life, using my Native American friend to do His will for His glory, setting up my testimony for the future. And God was also working in Chap, as well. The fact that he remembered my story meant more to me than I can say.

Some friends listen and remember what you talk about, but most do not. Some just forget.

Where could you ever find a pack of smokes from 1945? I mean, really. How would you find cigarettes from that long ago? Okay, I know you probably could, on the internet. This cigarette experience was before the internet was what it is today. I say near impossible to find a pack from that long ago, not opened. God can do the impossible.

You might say, "Buster, I do not want a pack of smokes from 1945."

LOL. I know it was just for me back then and for you to read about now, from Chap to me, set up by an awesome God.

God knew Chap was going to deliver my smoke signals. God just needed to put him in the old, abandoned farmhouse at the right time, so he'd find the smokes, remember my story, and save them for me to come back from California someday. That is not hard for God. I could never have got them without the Lord's help.

Another mystery, another piece of the puzzle; the picture was becoming clearer, slipping into my life, building one piece at a time to my story of the unbelievable ways the Lord uses people, numbers, and time to show He can draw His children to Himself, in ways we could never think of.

The point is, Jesus will do what it takes to put His plan in motion. Keep in mind too that His ways are not our ways. Our timing is not always His. It would have been easier for me if the Lord told me what He wanted in one day rather than twenty-five years of things adding up to what it did. When God speaks, His word does not come back void. Jesus used a number, like a hook in my mouth, bringing me to Himself. God could line up the planets as big as Jupiter if He wants to or something as small as a pack of cigarettes or an envelope for me to get in the future, before I was even born.

God is mysterious and invisible, doing things and giving signs and wonders in supernatural ways. Most people cannot think on those terms. Some will say the number means nothing to them; I understand that.

If you doubt God's power, you could be stopping your miracles from coming to pass in your life.

- 28 -
DREAMS OF FIGHTING

I stayed around Sisseton long enough to get into two different bar fights. Some guys in town must not have heard I was a scrapper. They wanted to know what I was made of. So with my mix of strength, youth, and speed, I gave them spankings. Looking back, I even shock myself in my fights because some of the guys I beat up were supposed to be tough.

You better be good at what you do if you decide to mess with me (when I was younger, that is). Because I was not an easy fight.

I was getting out of Sisseton. I felt the West Coast fever again and ended up going to Oregon to visit Julie, Joe's widow. My sister-in-law had moved up to McMinnville, Oregon, and invited me to come and stay if I wanted to. She left California not too long after my brother passed away. I liked it in that area, so I got a job up there at a tow company and body shop.

Around this time, I had a reoccurring dream of fighting three or four Mexicans at a time, in three different dreams. In one dream, I was in a house; I picked up a chair and was fighting with it, holding them back, but it was always at least three of them attacking me. I even told the guys at work I kept having this dream where I was fighting two or three Mexicans. We laughed about it.

Well, a couple weeks later, on a Sunday night, Ronda and I were shooting pool in the local sports bar in McMinnville. There were three pool tables, and we were having a beer.

I saw three Mexicans walk in, and I told Ronda, "Here they come."

She said, "Stop it, you always say this."

She knew about the dreams I had been having. I said to her, "Watch, they will come to our table."

She said, "No, they won't."

One of the guys walked over to our table and said, "Get off our table, boy."

I said, "Who you calling boy, boy?"

The one they called Poncho started to rush me on my left. I turned and smacked him on top of his head with my cue stick. He fell back, and the other two rushed me. I ended up at the bottom of a pile, and others in the bar got into the pile too. I was at the bottom, not getting hurt, just amazed about how fast it all happened.

The bartender began peeling the people off, and after about five minutes, the cops showed up; they took me to jail for aggravated assault with a deadly weapon, although they attacked me.

We got a copy of the police report, which said, "And for no reason, Mr. Buster whacked Poncho in the head with a cue stick, and the fight started."

It cost me a thousand dollars for an attorney to keep me out of jail. My attorney settled with the Mexicans, calling it a civil compromise, whatever that meant. I only had to go to jail Sunday night through Monday morning. I assume the charges were dropped.

- 29 -
THE LORD CONTROLS TIME

Ronda stayed with me about a year, then she started drinking and doing dope while I was at work. Our relationship was going down fast. The fighting started, so she went back to the reservation.

Ronda called me from Sisseton a couple months later to tell me her ex-boyfriend had murdered a guy. The police questioned Ronda because earlier that day, she was at the trailer where the murder took place. These people were drinking, and she said after she left, her ex-boyfriend and his friend must have killed another guy who was drinking with them. They tried cutting his body up to put it in plastic bags. Yeah, it was sick.

Gloria's brother, Babe, said he went over there that day to party. He knocked on the door, but they would not let him in. Babe said they probably were in the middle of cutting him up.

So now I was single again and could spend more time with my nephews. I am Uncle Buster, like on my blue envelope from God: "Ted's first haircut by Uncle Buster, 1945."

My daughter was staying with my mom in Dublin and going to school. The plan was after the school year was over, she would come to Oregon to live with me again. I found a house to rent in Sheridan, Oregon. I went to pick her up soon after school was out.

"Membership Card"

A boy named Bobby was sweeping floors at a shop I worked at in McMinnville. He heard I lived in Sheridan, and he needed a ride home one day, so I gave him a ride; he lived about half a block away from me. We became friends.

One day, he was at my house visiting and told me he wanted a picture I had, and would I be interested in trading for some old Cub Scout stuff he had. He said he could see I liked old stuff, so I said, "Bring it down and let me see what you have."

He had a Cub Scout hat, some pins, and a membership card; I asked him where he got them. He said the lady across the street from him was taking the stuff to Goodwill and asked if there was anything he wanted before she took it, so he took the scout stuff. Well, yes, I ended up with it and gave him the picture he liked. The card had 1946 on it, and I did not open it up until about a month later. I opened the card and saw 1945. Wow. Nice surprise. The Lord said this was another thing to add to my collection of stuff.

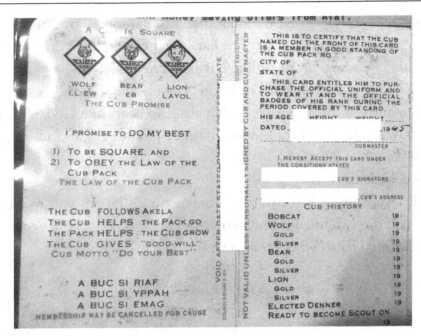

"Inside Membership Card"

My daughter and I went to South Dakota and picked up my son, because Gloria said, "Come get him; he needs his daddy." I was happy.

After I got back from South Dakota, I started seeing a lot of commercials on TV about the psychic hot line. The first five minutes were free. When you hear the beep, hang up, or you get charged every minute after the first five minutes. I called the number like eight different times through the month and hung up every time I heard the beep.

During one of the calls, the guy said, "Buster, I am going to give you fifteen more minutes free, so do not hang up when you hear the beep."

I almost felt like I hit the lotto. Yippy; but he lied; that call alone cost me seventy-four dollars. The company charged me for every one of the calls for a total of a hundred twenty-four dollars. Yes, I got ripped off. I should have known better.

I called the line because of the feelings I was having inside. I cannot really describe them, other than I knew something big was happening in my life. I needed to keep searching, and at that point, I turned to a pack of liars, scammers and liars from TV. The good thing is, God can take a bad thing and make it a good thing if He wants to use it for His glory.

This was in 1997, before people started wising up to the lies and scams on TV. I was angry to no end. I called the sheriff over to report a rip-off. He came to my house, and I told him I was lied to over the phone. He laughed and said I needed to get a lawyer if I wanted to do anything. Yeah, right; I felt stupid too. Then after about an hour of being mad, I looked down to the middle of the phone bill, and it said, I quote, "Note! You have saved $19.45 with AT&T." Bam! Bang! Pow!

The Lord spoke to me at that moment, like rain falling all over me.

God said, "Why call them? They are liars. You can find the truth in the Bible. I told you that ten years ago up in Billings. Read your Bible."

I said, "But Lord, I tried to read it. I don't understand it."

I was in the spirit, at that moment, in that place, to hear from God. He said, "Buster, can you see how I was in control of time, in your phone calls and adding it up to the number $19.45?"

"Yes, Lord," I said.

God said, "And how I can use this moment to enlighten you to My unlimited power?" He said the psychic hot line people are liars. Again, the message was "Read your Bible, Buster. That is where the truth is."

NOTE: You have saved   19.45

"ATT bill"

- 30 -
DAY OF SURRENDER

I picked up that old Bible and tried to read it again, but I just did not understand it. I said, "Lord, can you send someone to help me?" I did not hear anything back from Him right then.

I was living in a two-bedroom house but now needed a three-bedroom house for me and the kids. So I started looking around. I asked my current landlord, and he said he had one to rent two blocks over on the river. Cool. We moved in and loved it.

Not too long after moving in, on November 13, 1997, Promise Keepers Million Man March was going on in Washington DC. I was talking to God, and I was in the spirit. I had all my 1945 coins, envelope, smokes, and stuff out in my hand, spread out on my bed, and was talking to God.

I said, "Lord, it's awesome how You put together the things in time through the years and have answered more prayers than I can remember. You have been faithful to me, Lord. I have been bad in return, but you have never given up on me. This day, Lord, I promise to surrender my life to you if you give me one more sign with 1945. I will serve you to the day I die."

I was asking God for more understanding about what He wanted of me; I wanted just one more thing to lock in a surrender deal. I wanted one more sign with 1945. I knew He wanted me to read my Bible at the time, but I wasn't sure why.

The next day, I woke up and went to work; when I was there about five minutes, I was grabbing a tool out of my boss's toolbox. I had never seen anything but tools, but this fine morning, a nickel caught my eye. I walked away, but that voice said the nickel was a 1945. I said, "Yeah, right."

No, really, it is, I thought. *Go look.* So I went back over to the toolbox, opened the drawer, and picked it up. Yes, it was a 1945.

That voice said, "Buster, you promised God yesterday one more sign with 1945 and you would surrender your life to God. He will be your King."

Yes, I did. I may have been a thief, liar, and punk, but I kept my word to God, the best I could.

I fell to my knees and prayed to God, "I surrender to you, Lord God. Help me. I do not know much about churches. I don't even know how to pray right, but I want to serve you."

I asked if He could send someone to help me understand the Bible, because I knew He wanted me to read it. And from that day forward, I could see things around me happening like never before. In the world and in me spiritually, something big was happening.

It seemed like friends and family were acting a little different to me. After I surrendered to God, I could feel a change happen inside, like a new way to live growing in me. When I was around people and talking to them, I needed to learn how to talk to them again. It was like I was disconnected from them somehow. I was being reprogrammed.

A couple days later, I got an envelope in the mail from my old address. I could see it was not mine by the name; it was addressed to someone named Brenda. I opened it, and there was a check in it to the person who moved into my old house. At first, I thought I could cash this at the bar downtown; they cash anything. Then I thought I should walk it over to my old house, which was only two blocks over. That's what I did.

I knocked on the door; a woman opened it, and I said her mail came to my house. "Sorry, I opened it before I realized it was not for me. It was delivered to my house by mistake."

She said, "Thank you, you are so nice. Do you belong to a church?"

I said, "No."

She asked me if I wanted to go to a Bible study with her and her son that evening. I said okay.

I was thinking God set me up with this girl to help me understand the Bible, like I asked Him to. I met her later at a small building they were using for Bible study. About fifteen people were there, a small group from all around the state. They all seemed like nice people.

The name of their church is the Remnant. They worship the Sabbath on Saturday, the seventh day of the week, not Sunday, as the holy day of worship. The Fourth Commandment says to keep Saturday set apart for worshipping God. I did not know what God's Sabbath Day was until I met these people. Most of the Remnant people came out of the Seventh-day Adventist church. I worship God every day now.

So I told them about my 1945 deal, but nobody said much. I was used to that. It was really between God and me; nobody ever heard of a testimony like mine.

I could feel the Holy Spirit working in my flesh and in my spiritual self. Normally, the only time I felt the spirit move like this is when 1945 would majestically appear with a word of knowledge.

Breaking bad habits can be hard, like losing weight or old friends who do not help you live better. Making better choices can help you feel better and look better.

When I talk to other believers about God or my testimony, I can feel the Spirit of God moving inside. When two or more people gather in His name, He is there. There is normally a message that comes with this feeling or just a good boost of fire for the Lord. Sometimes, I will ask if anyone else felt the spirit moving, and most of the time, people say yes. I was beginning to understand the things God was doing, but not so much what I was doing.

In this Bible study, I told them I thought God told me to read my Bible, but I did not understand it, so I never read it. One of them said, "Let us pray that God opens His Word up to Buster, giving him understanding of God's Word, in Jesus's name we pray."

I wondered why they were using "in Jesus's name"; I didn't say anything about it then, but I still thought that Jesus was a fairy tale.

This Bible study was like a camp meeting study; it lasted three hours, and then we'd go to someone's house and have lunch together. This lasted a week. Some people came from out of state. I definitely felt a strong love with them that I never felt before, after they prayed for God to open His Word up to me. Now when I read the Bible, I have better understanding and can see things in the spirit. It worked; after the Bible study was over, the following weeks, I continued worshipping and reading the Bible with a small group.

- 31 -

I SAW THE LIGHT OF JESUS

After this Bible study was over, I was at home reading the Bible by myself and made a discovery. I was reading the book of Acts, chapter 9, and I got to verse 5 (NIV): "I am Jesus, whom you are persecuting." Wow, I saw Jesus there. For the first time, Jesus was not Santa Claus's baby. I was beginning to get it. The truth of the voice who was talking to me since I was a little boy. It hit me hard; a light came on. The Bible says if you fall on the Rock, you are broken. But if the Rock falls on you, you are crushed. I just fell on the Rock of my salvation. And it felt so good, I cried like a baby for like twenty minutes.

I saw my Lord for the first time, in living color, in my mind's eye. The whole time, Jesus was real, the God of Israel. I just now got the revelation in the most powerful way. I know I already said it, and I am saying it again, because this is the big part everyone needs to see. If you miss this, you have missed 80 percent of the most important part of my testimony. My book means almost nothing if you miss this.

The Word of God, Jesus, the Word made flesh, name above all other names given in heaven and on earth by which a person can be saved: Jesus.

Acts chapter 9 is Saul's testimony of his conversion on the road to Damascus. In short, Saul saw the light of Christ. I saw the same light, and it opened my eyes to Jesus! Wow. I sure hope you see how this is big for anyone who does not see Jesus as Lord. You must read Acts chapter 9, and I hope it does for you what it did for me and Saul. I realize some of you readers may already know this. But if not, read the Bible. Study the Bible with people who understand it and pray for understanding.

I am not saying this right. Before that moment, I did not believe Jesus was real. Saul did not believe Jesus was Lord, either. But he did believe in the God of Israel. He was a Jewish believer. It finally started to make sense, and it finally sunk in deep inside me. Saul saw the light of Jesus.

Saul had been hunting down Christians to throw them into jail for their execution. Saul had never met Jesus. He kept the commandments of God but did not believe Jesus was Lord. On his trip to Damascus, he saw the light of Jesus.

Lord, you set me up to discover in your Word that you were my God, Jesus. You are so awesome. I feel like more truth and light suddenly filled my soul, like in Acts chapter 2:1 (NIV), the day of Pentecost. It was me, Saul, and the Lord Jesus on the road to Damascus.

When I read Acts chapter 9, the Lord showed Himself to me like He did with Saul. That is how I found out Who Jesus was, and a mystery was revealed to me. I was on the road to Damascus with Saul personally. You have got to love how the Lord sets things up to see something. Again, that is another way you know when He is speaking to you. He does things you cannot think of to open you up inside. His ways cannot be duplicated by people, religion, or fake gods.

Please read the whole chapter to find out all of it; there is lots more in the chapter of Acts 9. In short, Saul was on the road to Damascus, with a couple other people. He was suddenly blinded.

From all around him, Saul heard a voice saying, "Why are you persecuting Me, Saul?"

Saul said, "Who are you, Lord?"

"I am Jesus."

Right then, the light blinded Saul, but he saw Jesus for the first time, like I did by reading about his experience. Saul became a believer and followed Jesus from that day forward.

Saul was taken to a Christian's house to be healed. They prayed over him, and his sight was returned after three days of being blinded. Saul knew now that Jesus is the Jewish Messiah, the King. People had been waiting for thousands of years for the Lamb of God to come. He came in the flesh and is still here alive in spirit. Read your Bible, people; preachers do not always get the Spirit of God to move, but the Bible always works, if you believe.

Saul began standing up for Jesus and was seen as a traitor to the Jews, a sell-out to the people of God in that day. The Jews caught up to Saul after his conversion. Scripture talks about the Jewish people beating Saul down because he was trying to preach about Jesus. They probably would have killed Saul, but a Roman soldier saw that he was being beaten by the Jews. Just so you know, Jesus' first twelve disciples were Jews. Not all Jews hated Jesus. So the Roman soldier stepped in to rescue Saul.

Romans kept order on the streets, like the police in our country. Romans had their own gods. They did not pray to Jesus or the Jewish God Jehovah, God of Israel, Father of Abraham, Isaac, and Jacob. Jewish laws did not apply to Roman laws. So Saul lived on to preach and spread the Gospel of Jesus.

God gave Saul a new name; he was now the great apostle Paul. Paul became one of the New Testament's greatest writers. He started out in life as a Jew, not believing in Jesus. Paul had never seen Jesus in person or heard Him preach. Saul hunted down Christians and cast them into prison before he saw the light of Jesus. I am sure Paul heard about Jesus but did not have any personal contact with Him. This was probably part of God's plan, to give him an experience first before setting him into play for Jesus, like me and maybe you.

So my spiritual life got stronger after discovering Jesus was God in the flesh. If you read John 1, it talks about the Word becoming flesh and walking among us. Until that moment, even after going to Bible study for a week, it did not click in my mind that Jesus was a real person, even God. I finally understand and believe in Jesus. I was thirty-seven years old before I realized that truth, and the truth will set you free.

The Jews killing Jesus was another Old Testament prophecy come true. Jesus had to die on the cross to keep God's Word true. Everything has been prophesied about this in God's Word. This is another way we can believe it is the truth, written by men inspired by God. His Word proves itself to be true over time.

- 32 -
MY TESTIMONY GOES OUT

A couple years earlier, Julie, my sister-in-law, introduced me to Brenda. Brenda was from Walnut Creek, California. She lived in the same area of Oregon. We were friends, and one day not long after my conversion of the knowledge of Christ, Brenda came over to my house to visit; I started preaching the Good News to her, and she received Jesus as Lord that day. Looking back now, I am so glad I was bold and did not hold back, because a couple years later, Brenda passed away. God bless her soul. I am sure she is in heaven.

The same day Brenda was over and I was leading her in the sinner's prayer, another friend of mine, Brandon, was sitting there, watching and listening to us. He told me a couple months later that he received Jesus that day too. He agreed with us, inside. Amen.

I think Brandon was too macho to talk to me about it, but later, he came over to the house and said he had an experience with God.

I said, "I did not know you believed in God."

I asked him what his experience was. He said he was fishing in the river, walking in the water, and slipped on the rocks. He thought he broke his leg. He said it was so painful. That night, while lying in bed, he reached up to the sky and asked Jesus to heal his leg. He said he felt like he was vibrating, and a warm feeling came over him, and his leg was healed by the next day. Praise the Lord.

Around the same time, my daughter came over with two of her girlfriends, and one of their mothers was visiting. I asked them if they wanted to see what God had done for me. They said yes, so I showed them my documents I had in a folder, along with my testimony. I told them how it all came down, like I am doing in this book.

After I was done telling my story, Rachel, one of the girls, got up, walked over to her mother, and said something I could not hear, and they suddenly left. The next day, the mom came back to my house and asked, "What did you do to my daughter last night?"

I said, "What? You were sitting right there. I told them my testimony about how Jesus came into my life. Why, what happened?"

She said Rachel cried all the way back home to McMinnville (about a twenty-minute drive).

I did not know what to say. She left, and I went to the Lord in prayer and asked, "What happened, Lord?"

He said, "The little girl believed your testimony, and her heart opened, and Jesus went in. Go now and keep preaching the Good News."

I am so glad I was bold in preaching Jesus that night because Rachel received Jesus and was saved. The sad part, bless her soul, she passed away a couple years later.

We serve an awesome God because she received the Good News before it was too late. Saint Paul said be bold in Christ Jesus. Amen.

For a while, I didn't write this book because I thought it was too hard for people to understand. It's just too much. I concluded that God asked me to write the book, and He is drawing His children into the knowledge of Himself and His salvation plan. I hope those who read this book call on the name of Jesus and get saved. Ultimately, it is up to God whether people get saved or not: "Here is the patience of the saints; here are those who keep the commandments of God and the faith of Jesus" (Revelation 14:12 (NIV)).

I need to stay focused and finish the job I started, and let God do the rest.

- 33 -
BROKEN BONES OF UNBELIEF

I was living in the house on the river, and this is the lease agreement from the house at the time. In the middle of the document is my number, showing when the house was built. I wish I could have bought that house. My son caught his first fish on the river behind the house.

YEAR BUILT *1945*

"Rental Contract"

After I discovered Jesus was Lord, learning was easier. My memory increased as well. The more I read His Word, the more I could understand His plan of salvation. It was unfolding inside me, and the world cannot take that away from you. I realize how important God's Word is now to everyday life.

One of my daughters and my son were living with me. My daughter was in high school, and my son was in second grade. He said he remembers me picking him up from daycare with the Harley. It always made him feel cool, he said.

Gloria came to Sheridan to visit and liked it, so she rented a house a couple miles down the road from us. She only stayed a couple months and then moved back to SD with three of our girls.

I had some rough days, but for the most part, I had a nice awakening for the first couple months. It was like a new journey of enlightenment with Jesus. Before knowing Who Jesus was or that He was God, I felt like I knew God, but I could only get so close to Him. It was like there was a part missing or there was something keeping us from getting closer. And I was right. Jesus is the bridge to the Father. Jesus is our mediator. Jesus covers our sins so we can approach the Father. God is holy, and we cannot get close to Him without the blood of Christ covering us. We can pray and be close to God, but we must be glorified before we get to heaven. Heaven is a holy place where sin and evil cannot be. Sin and evil are like a virus that can infect anyone who gets too close to it. After we receive Jesus as Lord, we do get glorified before we enter the holy place with God. For now, we get a covering of Jesus's blood so we can get the benefits of belonging to the Father God. They are one: Father, Son, and Holy Spirit. Jesus said if you have seen Him, Jesus, you have seen the Father.

I called my mom to tell her I found Jesus in my life. She said, "Yeah, right." Then we argued a little about nothing, and she hung up on me. I thought my mom would be happy for me.

I called Julie, my sister-in-law, to tell her I was saved. She laughed at me like my mom did. She started some kind of negative attitude, and we hung up kind of mad, for some reason.

I wondered what was going on.

A couple days later, I was going to call my friend Don. We ride Harleys together. He's like a brother, and I thought he'd understand me. I called Don and told him I was coming over to tell him something.

He said, "Sure, Buster, come on over."

I wanted to tell him the good news that I found and received Jesus into my life.

When I got to Don's house, I said, "God used that number 1945 to speak to me again."

But Don was like a grumpy old man. As soon as I started to tell him, and he saw my Bible, he said he did not want to hear what I was going to tell him. That really hurt me; it hurt my feelings, and we began to argue loudly.

My son was with me in Don's kitchen, and I said, "Son, go to the car and wait for me." He walked out, and I said, "Don, you blankety blank!"

He said some hateful things to me, and I had about enough of his disrespectful mouth, so I said, "Get up, you blankety-blank."

We were going to rock and roll in his kitchen, but he saw in my eyes the pain he would soon feel if he got up from the table. I am glad he did not get up. He always talked a big game. Don was a logger by trade, with a bigger mouth than me, and that was not easy to do, even after I met Jesus. I can admit it has taken me twenty-five years, walking as close as I can with Jesus, and my temper is only a little better, but I have not given up trying to grow to be like Jesus. It is a lifetime commitment and full of struggles, and until God glorifies me, I will be human, with lots of weaknesses and faults. I do believe I am much better than I was without Jesus as my Lord.

So I left Don's house, hurt, confused, and weakened inside. I even prayed before I went over there to tell him about my unbelievable story of how God drew me to Himself for a relationship and my redemption.

What I did not know was God was working on Julie, my mom, and Don behind the spiritual curtains.

A few days later, my mom called me and asked if I would pray for her leg. She fell off the couch and fractured her leg. I said yes, I would pray for her leg.

A couple days later, Julie called me next, from the hospital, crying and asking me to pray for her leg. She fell and broke her kneecap and cut her artery. It did not look good for her leg, she said. They might have to amputate because she lost a lot of blood to her leg. I prayed for her.

A couple days later, Don called me from the hospital and said he had a wreck on his Harley. He broke his leg and collarbone but otherwise was okay; he asked me to pray for him. He said maybe God saved him for something, and he was sorry for causing a scene at his house a couple weeks earlier.

I really did not know what was going on, all in the same month. They acted mad at me because I got saved, then they all called for me to pray for them. Of course, if you were to ask them, they would not remember this. Very few people remember what I am talking about with my God stuff, but I do. There are medical records that prove my stories are true. Why do I need to prove everything? Because I can; remember that.

Keep in mind, believing by faith is a big part of how God operates in His salvation plan. Bottom line, believing in the shed blood of Christ on the cross is another part of what must happen in the plan of salvation for humankind. Believing the Word of God is real is another part of the plan. Believing by faith is another important part.

Read Hebrews 11, the whole chapter. If you don't read things out of God's Word, the Bible, you are missing the most important parts I am sharing. Look at it like this: When I say something to you, it is just hearing from a man. When you read from the Bible, you now have heard it from God Himself.

Do not forget before reading to ask the Lord to open His Word up to you, giving you understanding.

Doing this can save you years of time, wondering how to get closer to God. Reading the Bible equals wisdom and knowledge and life. Do not be lazy; get your Bible out.

Romans 4:3 (NIV) says Abraham believed God, and God counted him as righteous because of his faith.

Romans 10:17 (NIV) says faith comes by hearing the messages of God.

By the second call, I was wondering if God was doing something here. After Don called me, I knew God was working on three people close to me, and, yes, on myself, teaching us how Jesus operates on people who are in our lives. Three badly hurt legs, not just a bump: two broken bones, and my mom's leg was fractured.

So I asked God if He punished them. He said no, that after they rejected me, it was like they rejected Him. He said He removed His hand of protection from them, and they hurt themselves. The Lord said, "Buster, I am your protector. I guide your every step in life, and I am ready to catch you when you fall."

In Genesis 32:25-29 (NIV), Jacob wrestled with God until the sun came up.

We all wrestle with God at some point in our lives, don't we? Jacob said he saw the face of God that night; God popped Jacob's hip out of joint so he would remember God every step of his life from that day forward. The Lord blessed him, and at some point in their relationship, God gave him a new name, Israel. And now you know how Israel got her name, by the God of Israel, Father of Abraham, Isaac, and Jacob. You would have to read the whole story about Jacob to understand some of what I just told you.

I was like, wow, what an awesome God we have. I was beginning to understand how He works through me and others around me. I am still learning every day to be a better person, and I learn more about Jesus and how He does things. No one can know the depths of His protection, love, mercies, power, and grace.

- 34 -
MY LAST FIGHT

Being a Christian was new to me. I got baptized ten years earlier but walked away after going to church two or three Sundays.

Some of you may not know what the Sabbath means. The Fourth Commandment in the Bible says on the seventh day of the week, you must keep the day holy; you must not work but rest in the Lord God and worship Him forever (Hebrews 4 (NIV)).

But after some time, people decided to change the day of worship that God commanded from Saturday to Sunday. The Sunday Christian churches call it the Lord's day. It has its purpose. It is good to worship the Lord every day.

The subject of the Sabbath is a controversy to the world to this day. Sunday or Saturday can be a big distraction to preaching the Gospel of Jesus. I let the controversy distract me for a few months; don't let it distract you. It was part of where the Lord took me, part of my teaching, and I had to find the place of my rest in Jesus. This controversy had to be dealt with. I do believe the Lord wanted me to understand the Old Testament and His Ten Commandments first.

I worshipped and studied for a couple months with the Remnant church, a break-off from the Seventh-day Adventist church. After a while, this church, the people, and the laws just became too much for me. Was the Sabbath truth? Yes.

I met a guy named Bob; he was a contractor. I purchased a lot in town, and Bob was building a shop for me on the lot. I was going to give him one of my Harleys for building the shop; he too was a Sabbath keeper, not from the Remnant church but from the United Church of God. We had some good times together, and I went to his church for a while too. I miss Bob. I lost his number after moving out of Oregon.

Julie, my daughter, finally graduated high school; an old boyfriend from South Dakota came out to visit her, and he talked her into moving back to Sisseton. So it was just my son and me now.

One evening, Bob came over, and we ended up at a bar in Sheridan. Bob was about six foot two, 220 pounds, and a good athlete in school. He was strong, not a shrimp like me (I'm five foot, seven and at the time weighed 185 pounds; big threat, right?).

So these four guys decided to start a fight with us, for no real reason other than we may have been better looking than them. Bob and I cleaned their clocks. It was broken tables and smashed faces, spilled drinks, and hurt feelings. The police came, but we did not go to jail because people said Bob and I didn't start the fight. The bartender had kicked those guys out earlier. They came back in to meet their fate of a bloody face. We kicked their behinds.

While we were talking to the police, the Lord spoke inside me, saying, "Buster, that was your last fight." He said He was going to do my fighting for me from now on. The Lord said the next fight I got into was not going to turn out good for me, and I said, "What?" Sad face. He was very clear.

So I kept walking with Jesus, and I tried to spread the message of the Good News. I found out lots of people did not want to hear whatever I was talking about. One time, someone said my preaching and delivery were all wrong. Thank you; I think as time goes on, a person begins to develop a way to preach, a kind of style, you might say, and it takes time and practice to do it so people like it. I did learn that the Lord is the One Who does the saving, and it is His spirit and power, not mine, that draws a person to Himself.

I was thinking about me not having a good delivery on preaching and thought Jesus preached His messages perfectly, and the people still killed him. So it could be the people too, not just the delivery of the truth, right?

If people want to know God, they will search for Him or listen to others who have a relationship with Jesus. Let the Spirit of God move because His love is one of the powers that saves us. Teachers and preachers play a part in God's salvation plan. God's Word will be preached, and hearing the Word preached leads us to our salvation (Romans 10:17 (NIV)).

There for a while, I thought finding things with 1945 from God was over. In 1997, my awakening to the truth of Jesus was not over; there would be more things coming.

I prayed, thanking the Lord for blessings and good things before they even came. I was praying for people, and the Lord was answering a lot of my prayers because He is faithful to His people.

Y2K was approaching, and I was falling for all the hype that the 2000 computer glitch would crash computers and start doomsday. So in the summer of 1999, my son and I moved back to South Dakota to be close to all the other kids and family. I found a house in Watertown, fifty miles south of Sisseton. Watertown is on the southeast corner of the Sisseton reservation.

Right away, I went out for a beer in downtown Watertown; seems I get thirsty in SD. I was there ten minutes, and some guy tried to start a fight with me; I'm used to that. This guy walked over to the booth where my friend and I were sitting and started talking baloney to me. I got up out of my seat and told the bartender this guy was bothering us, and he went and sat back down.

The friend I was with said, "His name is Rugged Man. He just got out of prison and is crazy, so do not fight him."

I said, "Dude, I did not want to fight him."

Rugged Man came over again and said to me, "I think you better be leaving."

He looked really intimidating. He was a half-breed, the worst kind when it comes to being in a fight because they had to fight whites and Indians to find their place in life on the reservation. He was not tall but looked very strong, and I could see that because he was wearing a tank top. His hair blond was greased back, and he had black eyeliner on. He looked like a walking, talking, demon to me, really. He did pump some fear into me, I must admit. Gloria was half-white, and she went through the half-breed stuff too; it makes you tough.

I slid out of the booth where I was sitting, and he walked away from me, so we did not fight. I was thinking that the Lord told me a year earlier, no more fighting, and the next one was not going to turn out well for me. That would have been my next fight.

About a year later, another friend called me and said he was trying to stop a fight someone got in with Rugged Man. This guy's hand got cut, and his friend was stabbed to death. Rugged Man ended up back in prison for murder.

God warned me of fighting in my last fight at the bar in Sheraton, Oregon, saying He would do my fighting for me. He would be my protector, and to this day, in the year 2021, I have not been in a fight since (came close a couple times). I am sixty-one now, so I am feeling my age and know how to walk away better, thank God. I do think I am good for one three-minute round, at least for a couple more years; remember that, Chumley.

- 35 -
BLUE-EYED GIRL

A couple months later, Sarah, my girlfriend, got pregnant. We broke up two weeks before she found out she was having a baby. My youngest baby girl was my sixth child. All my kids are registered tribal members in Sisseton Wahpeton Tribe, and I am so proud of all of them.

I heard Sarah did not want to keep this baby, because she had a couple kids already, and it was hard for her. Then I heard through the grapevine that Sarah's uncle and aunt wanted a baby. It is not that uncommon for babies to be given to other family members to raise. If her uncle ended up with my baby girl, I was okay with that, but I wanted to raise her myself. So I called my mom and asked her if she would help me raise my youngest baby, if I could get her. She said yes, so I asked Sarah if I could have her.

She said no, the baby was going to her uncle. I think Sarah did not want me to take her out of state to California; sad face. I was glad in one way; she would be raised Indian. I think it is a good thing for her to know her roots on her mother's side.

I pulled my back out of place, and it was hurting more than the first time it was hurt. I was not working because of my back, so my money was running out. I started selling my stuff, including my 1928 Chevy hot rod truck. I was still buying and selling autos and bikes, but I was not making enough money to pay rent and food, so I did not put up a fight trying to get my baby. I was sad for the most part. I would have raised her. I went to get an attorney, but they wanted a ten thousand dollar retainer to start the process. I was almost broke. Just recently, in the past couple years, my baby girl has reached out to me, and we have started talking. That is good. She is nineteen now.

I started looking online for a girlfriend and found one. It was like it was meant to be. We both loved Jesus. I ran an ad looking for a woman who loved Jesus. Kathy responded. She lived in South Carolina. Not long after meeting her, I got a call from my mom that her husband Ted had passed away. What? Another shock. My mom said she was going to bring him back to South Dakota to be buried with his family on the reservation. I was already in SD, so a couple days after Ted's funeral, my plan was to go back to California to help my mom, but first I would go to South Carolina to see if my new girlfriend was real or just a fantasy.

So I made it to South Carolina. I stopped for three days and found out Kathy liked to drink too much. I asked her a couple times online if drinking was a problem for her, and she said no. I told her I was done with the drinking thing. I had enough of that with my last couple girlfriends. Kathy lied to me or just did not think it was a problem, so I left her house and headed back to California.

Ted was more like a good friend to me than a dad. My little brother looked up to Ted like a dad. Ted got sick. He had fluid in his lungs and an infection, and passed away. He was too young at fifty-four years old.

On my way back to California, I was talking to God, somewhere in Wyoming on Interstate 80 going west.

I said, "Lord, I would like to find a girl with blue eyes to love."

Clear as day, the Lord said, "You already know her, Buster."

Okay, I was thinking and thinking, not saying a lot, but I was thinking, *Who, Lord? I cannot think of any blue-eyed girls I know.*

Not another word from God about it; I could not figure out who He was talking about.

After getting to California, Kathy kept calling me; I called her too, and she asked if she could come to California and see me. I said okay. She came, and we got married the day after she got there, and on the third day, I said I wanted a divorce. LOL. After we got married, we went to San Francisco to have dinner, and yes, we started drinking again. Kathy was not like most girls I had been with. She said she could see demons and spirit creatures, and she was not kidding. I was okay with that because I knew demons were real, and she seemed to have it all under control, but after we started drinking, like in South Carolina, something strange started to happen to the good time. After a couple shots and a couple beers, we walked down the street to another bar. We went inside, got a beer, and walked over to the fireplace area to sit down.

She stopped and turned to me and said, "Who are you?"

Wow, like a burst of heat or fire passed into me, and a voice from inside of me said, "Knock that glass of beer out of her hand. Make it break on the brick fireplace."

Hello, this was not a joke. I was like, what is wrong with me? I felt like something was trying to use me to hurt her. I never told her what was going on inside me.

I just said, "Let's go back to our room, honey."

We got back to the room, and it felt like our love was being hijacked. She was jumping on the bed like a little kid. Our room was on the third floor, and I was next to the window.

I was on my knees, praying, "Lord, help me get through this night."

I did not know what was happening to us or me. Something said, "Throw the chair out the window; break the glass and jump out." Not funny, but kind of funny now. So we made it through the night, and in the morning, I said, "I want a divorce."

I think the demons followed her and waited for an opening to hurt her. That is my guess. I am not sure, but it was crazy stuff. I am glad I did not do anything to hurt her. I've had a little experience in dealing with drunks, which helped a little, and I prayed for help from Jesus. I was used to drunks trying to hit or hurt me; in this case, she was okay. It was me who was losing it. The next day, she got on the plane and went home. We did the paperwork, got a divorce, and that short story was over. Kathy suggested we get counseling, but I declined. I do feel like I learned about how demons can tempt me and operate in people, especially after drinking alcohol. That is the truth.

After getting back to California, my sister told me of a church she was going to. She said it was a cool place to worship, so I went to it. After church, there was a Bible study that I went to. I walked into the Bible study room after church and saw a woman with blue eyes. I completely forgot about what the Lord said about the blue eyes to me, going through Wyoming a couple weeks earlier. Plus, He said I already knew her. The thing is, I did not know Kim. So it could not have been her, and it did not matter anyway, I guess.

I thought, *I could marry this girl*. Six months later, Kim and I got married. I told her I wanted to get married on August 17 because that was my brother Joe's birthday, and it would make it easy for me to remember our anniversary, but Kim wanted to get married on another date.

She had two kids from her first marriage, and I had my son with me. Kim's boy was around eight, her daughter was around four, and it was hard blending the kids. They did not get along very well.

- 36 -
MY BURNING BUSH

After getting married, Kim and I moved into an apartment first and then into a house in Dublin, California. I was working at a body shop in Pittsburg, about thirty-five miles from Dublin. Kim worked in Pleasanton, close to our house.

We could not get a phone line installed in the house we moved into because a big bush was growing around the base of the telephone pole. It really bugged me that it was such a big deal; it should not have been that big of a deal. It was just a bush. The pole was on the neighbor's side of the fence, so I could not cut it myself. This went on for days. Nobody would cut the bushes. I was standing outside in the garage, looking out back at the pole and bush, and thought I could just burn the bushes. That would end the problem quick.

After thinking that, I heard that still small voice say "No, you better not do that. You could get into trouble and go to jail. Let God handle it."

That is what I heard. That is what the voice said to me. I was like, okay, right; God's going to come cut the bushes for me. Okay, I will let God handle it. I was sure what I heard; it was not like the first time hearing from Him. Of course, I did not tell my wife or anyone the kind of voices I heard because they would lock me up, I am pretty sure.

So I went back into the house, and we went to bed. About ten o'clock, the back yard lit up like the Fourth of July. No kidding. I looked out the window; I was only fifty feet from the power pole, and the transformer was exploding with sparks. It blew up and was spitting sparks out like crazy. The bushes twenty feet below started burning and were consumed.

Yay! Yippy! God took care of it for me. I do not think it was a coincidence because the Lord had been doing unbelievable stuff like this for me for a long time, and I am sure the fire truck call is still on record. I did not think the Lord would burn the bush by exploding the transformer, but He always seems to do something I had not thought of. I do know what was said to me, that's for sure.

Kim said I should I call the fire department; I said, "No, let it burn, baby."

I assume the neighbors called it in because the fire department came and put the fire out.

I never told Kim about the burning bush story because she was not a supernatural kind of girl.

She would have said, "Are you crazy?"

I would have said, "I think so." Another proof we really did not know each other very well.

After four years of marriage, Kim and I decided to divorce. I was not happy about getting a divorce; it happened kind of fast, and nobody was cheating. Kim was taking antidepressant pills after her divorce, before she met me, and she stopped taking them. A couple weeks later, I think she started having withdrawals. It threw her body all out of whack. She said she had bad anxiety because of her last husband. I did not see it because the pills kept it under control.

I said, "Maybe you do not even need them. I heard those pills were not good for your liver."

So she stopped taking them, and about two weeks later, everything just fell apart for us, too fast to stop. I prayed for healing in our marriage.

One night a year before this, we had one of the kid's friends over for dinner, and I started to talk about Jesus. Kim gave me the mean look and told me to stop talking. I had the feeling that night was the end of our marriage. If there is one thing that really bugs me, it is if I am talking about Jesus, and someone tells me to stop talking about God or Jesus. Mad face.

Kim went back to the doctors to get back on the pills, but it was too late. We were going to divorce.

I asked God, "What did I do wrong?"

He said, "First, you never asked me what I thought about marrying Kim, and second, you stopped loving her the way she needed to be loved."

I did not know that. I did not really know how to love, I guess. I was not loving my wife, family, or people in general very well. I needed God to help me with this love thing; I did not realize it. I knew how to hurt people. I asked God to help me learn to love people better. I think my heart was hardened by the world. So many fights and so much pain in my life hardened my heart and deadened me to love people properly.

- 37 -
LICENSE PLATE 1945

I had been working for Steve about four years when we divorced. Steve asked me to manage his shop, and I said okay. It was a body and paint shop. For extra money and to keep busy, we would buy wrecked cars from customers.

Steve had a friend who had a wrecked truck, so he brought it in to get an estimate. If it was totaled, we would buy it from him. The insurance claimed it to be totaled. It was a 1997 Chevy pickup, and Steve's friend did not want to repair it and asked Steve if he would buy it. Steve said we would buy it, but he was going through hard times, and money was tight, so he asked me if I wanted it. I said no at first because I wanted something newer, but Steve asked me again if I would buy it because he told his friend we would. I could fix it and sell it or keep it, so I bought it for Steve's low price.

A couple weeks later, we dug it out of the back of the shop where we parked the other wrecked vehicles. I moved the truck to the frame rack to start working on it, and Steve said, "Buster, is that the number you told me about?"

I looked at the license plate, and it had 1945 on it. I said, "Wow, thank you, Lord."

This truck really was for me. What a blessing. I was glad I bought it now and had my moment with God in the Spirit for a split-second, like I always do, when the number comes at me in a way that catches my attention.

I am sure God gave this to me to add to my story. At first glance, my thought was God could set me up on a license plate too, by making sure that after the truck got into a wreck, it made it to our shop. Everything had to be in place, like Steve had to be out of money, and I had to have the money ready to buy the truck, all at the right time. Nothing is too hard for the Lord. His timing is always perfect.

After repairing the truck and driving it for a while, I gave it to my brother, who needed a truck. I told him if he ever sold it to keep the plates for me. And I knew when he put the truck in his name, he would get new plates because one plate was missing. I was glad I took the one plate to add to my story. He knew about my 1945 thing and did not do what I asked. He said the DMV needed to take the plate on the truck, which was true. I thought he would take the plate off for me, but before I gave him the truck, I took the front plate off, to be sure I got at least one of them before he drove off. Right. People just do not hear me sometimes or just do not care, or both.

- 38 -
OUT OF BUSINESS

I was single a couple weeks. I put my name on a Classmates.com website for my high school, class of 1977 in Hayward. I just wanted to meet up with old friends in the area.

Not long after I put my name on the Classmate's website, Judy, my neighbor from across the street in Hayward, messaged me. Cool. I looked for her a couple times through the years because I always felt love for her. Whenever I was in the neighborhood and in between relationships, I asked a couple people where Judy ended up. Nobody knew, so I never did find her until now. I never really got over her.

Judy and I talked online a little and then decided to meet at the local coffee shop in Dublin, where I was still living. No, I did not move to South Dakota this time; after Kim and I got divorced, she moved out, and my son and I stayed in the house.

Judy and I met, had a cup of coffee, and talked about the past twenty-five years. We had a good time reminiscing about the old neighborhood and friends. She had three boys and a girl; I had five girls and a boy. My son was going to high school in Dublin. She said her daughter was still in school in Tracy, although she was buying a house in Stockton. Judy was getting a divorce too. She talked about how much of a drive it was from Stockton to Dublin to work every morning, so I asked if she wanted to rent a room from me, as I had an empty room.'

We met up again not long after that first visit, and she said she would take me up on the offer to rent a room, so she was closer to work. She had a very good job. Judy and her daughter soon moved in. At this time, the housing crash started in California, and she was trying to sell her house. It was so far from work for her, and after getting a divorce, it was too much to make her mortgage alone.

I did not know what Judy was thinking in the lines of a relationship because we both were getting a divorce. We had a good time as friends, and I tried not to get involved with her, although I did have feelings for her going back to high school. I did not make any moves on her, and she was not the aggressive type, or we would have been doing you-know-what. We slept in the same California king bed for months, just sleeping. We both worked very hard and fell asleep fast.

Judy's daughter Susie had a room, and my son had the other room. Judy and I shared a room. It was great having Judy as a friend first, for like seven months, without having sex right away.

Another good friend, Jerry, just moved back from Hawaii. Jerry was another friend from Hayward; he lived next door to me. I lived with him up in Portola, back in 1988. He built a house up in Oregon and asked me to come visit, so I did. I liked it up there.

Jerry said, "Buy a house here; they're cheap right now because of the housing crash."

I looked around and found a cute little two-bedroom house. I liked it and moved forward to purchase it. I was still working at the body shop in Pittsburg.

After returning from Oregon, I told Judy I was going to buy a house in Oregon. She helped me fill out the paperwork, but I didn't realize she was sad that I was moving soon. The body shop was not making much money because of the bad economy, and the guys at work started stealing material from the shop like sandpaper, tape, and other things to do side jobs. One of them told me they planned on putting Steve out of business so they could take over the shop. Steve had been there for thirty years.

I told Steve the guys were stealing from the shop and not doing their work on time. If it did not stop, the shop would have to close. I could not see how we could do it. I also told him that one of the illegal workers told me they were planning on taking over his shop. He laughed at me and said they were just messing with me.

The landlord was already giving us breaks on the rent because he could see it was getting tough. Shops all over the state were closing. I told the workers we needed to start conserving on materials more and get jobs out on time, or nobody would have a job. The illegals we had working for us started making up lies about me to get me fired because I was in their way. I was the one running the shop, and they began putting pressure on me because they wanted to take it over. It was getting ugly there.

I was on salary and working late nights, so not making more money, just trying hard to keep the doors open. I wanted to keep my job and help Steve make it.

I loved Steve as a friend and a boss. I had seen him go through so much pain while I worked for him. His fourteen-year-old daughter passed away with cancer. Not long after that, his wife wanted a divorce. Now these friends of his, the illegals we had working for us, started to bring the shop down to the ground.

Steve, who was a Mexican American, didn't believe me about the guys taking over his shop. I received a couple death threats, mixed with their lies, and it seemed like Steve was not backing me. He just did not believe what I told him they were doing.

Then, this lady friend of Steve's said she'd help him save the shop; she'd work for free and give Steve free sex too. I could not compete with that. I told Steve that before all the lies, hate, and stealing started, about two years ago, there were about seven illegals working for us. A couple workers were good and loyal to the shop, and they told me what was going on. They were the good ones. They did not steal anything and were not trying to bring the shop down. Eight years I was there; I saw different workers come and go. A couple of them were working for Steve when I started there; they were the bad apples in the group. Any time we hired new workers, the bad apples would infect the new workers, keeping the hate and lies alive in the shop. They were there after I left. For three years, I put up with their threats and hate, but I kept working because I liked Steve, and I do not scare easily. Being the manager was nice, other than babysitting the guys half the time. I never worked at a place longer than two years in my life because I moved around so much. Can you imagine that?

My loan for the house was approved, and my plan was to move to Oregon. I started preparing to move, then other things started to happen; to help Steve out, I was taking pay cuts. We took jobs, and the people did not want to pay their deductibles on their insurance; workers were still stealing, but it was not enough to keep the doors open. I finally left Steve's body shop.

After that, I didn't like illegals in America. My feelings are, please come here legally. We have laws. It helps law enforcement fight crime when we know who you are, so they can be held accountable like Americans are for our crimes.

Within a year or so, Steve closed the doors forever. The woman didn't really help much, and after that, the illegals took over on his lease. Their plan finally worked; they were in business. It hurt Steve, and it hurt me to see it happen to him. God closes one door and opens another. Amen.

- 39 -
CONFIRMATION ABOUT THE BLUE-EYED GIRL

My plans started to change about moving to Oregon, so I rented the house out. Judy and I started a relationship by then, and our friendship turned into a real strong love. It was so nice to be friends first because it led into a very good, solid, and close relationship. I have never had it like that. I always rushed into relationships. Being friends first, I think, made a big difference, and we both loved and trusted in Jesus. It was the strongest part of what we had; we are equally yoked together.

Judy and I were going to South Dakota to visit my kids, and we decided to get married in Reno as we were passing through. Unfortunately, it was late at night, so we decided to get married on our way back. We had a nice visit with the kids in South Dakota.

By now, we all had cell phones. When we got back to Reno, we were going to get married, but Judy's mom and dad called and said they were in the Bay Area. They were planning to leave Sunday to go back to Texas. It was Friday, so we decided to wait again on getting married; sad face. Judy told me later she thought I kept getting cold feet. I told her it was just the timing kept getting messed up somehow.

We got back to the Bay Area and visited with her parents. We saw my grandpa too.

Grandpa really liked Judy and said, "You guys should get married while Judy's parents are here."

I thought that was a great idea. It was Saturday, and Judy's dad said they would stay an extra day for us if we got married on Monday when the courthouse opened. We got married, and it wasn't until after we got married that I noticed the date: August 17, my brother Joe's birthdate. Yes, that was the date I wanted to get married before. Thank You, Jesus. The timing was perfect. We could not have planned it any better had we tried ourselves. To this day, I have never forgotten our anniversary.

About a year later, after getting married, I was just thinking about nothing, really; you know that time when you drift kind of out in space? Someone asks, "What are you thinking about?" And you say, "Nothing, really." You know you're thinking about something, but like a dream, you cannot remember the thoughts racing through your mind. Some thoughts are stupid, and other thoughts, nobody really wants to know about. Some thoughts don't even belong to you; they are implanted by hate or evil. It is all jumbled up thoughts, in that moment of time.

Well, I was in that kind of thought, and sometimes that is when I can hear from God the best, breaking through my space. On His time or the time He chooses to talk to me. He said, "Oh, Buster?"

"Yes, Lord?"

"Remember about five years ago, somewhere on that highway Interstate 80 going west through Wyoming? You asked me for a woman with blue eyes for your next love."

"Yes, Lord."

"And I told you, you already know her?"

"Yes, I remember."

"It was Judy."

"Wow, you were right again, Lord; she has blue eyes, and I didn't even remember you saying that until now. You are so awesome, Lord. You are absolutely good."

"Yes, Buster. I AM."

And this is a perfect example of when God gives you confirmation of a conversation that you had with Him in the past. "Lord, do you remember when I did not want to have a relationship with Judy at first? Mostly because I thought that I would just hurt her, because I am mean, and she deserves better. Lord, you told me you thought Judy would make the perfect wife for me and not to worry."

"I remember that."

"I said to you, if you teach me how to love her, I will marry her, because I love her too much to put her through my dysfunctional love. And you said you would teach me how to love and respect her. It has been the best marriage I ever thought possible. So nice, she takes care of me and my six kids and her four kids, and we have nineteen grandkids to date. I could not have done this without your help, Lord. Thank you."

We've been married eleven years now, and we have not had one blow-out fight. Yes, a couple disagreements, but no angry fights with bashing, cursing, and outbursts. I tell my friends and family this, and most of them laugh; they cannot imagine it's possible to have such a good marriage. I think they think I must be lying. Most of what I say can be proven.

But really, Judy loves me. She respects me. She is the best woman in the world for me. I love her so much, my brain cannot explain it.

"You were right, Lord. Judy helps me with everything. Without you, Lord, and Judy, this book may not have been finished. Without you and Judy in my life, I really do not know where I would be. Looking for a blue-eyed girl, riding down a long, lonely road on my Harley, smashing, breaking, fighting in a bar somewhere, in prison for hurting someone, or six feet under."

Judy and I work well together, and we have a good time whatever we do. She is working for the same company in Pleasanton. I take care of maintaining our three houses and do side jobs, paint motorcycles, body work, and buy and sell bikes and autos for some extra money. I also preach the Gospel of Christ on the side for free. We do not gamble, do drugs, or drink, so we don't spend lots of money on stupid stuff.

Our main house is in the mountains at three thousand feet, seventy miles south of Lake Tahoe in God's country. We love it up here, with lots of trees. The Lord has blessed us more than we thought was possible. Judy makes good money, which gives me more time to write books and fix things, paint, weld, and feed the animals. Life is good serving Jesus. We do not belong to a church yet, but we do go when invited to a church now and then. We have not found one church we really want to commit to. We are not religious; we just love Jesus and have a relationship with Him together. We do have a street ministry and try to help others in any way we can. Mostly, we share the Gospel and the Good News of Jesus.

We try to live a good, godly life and stay out of trouble. Most of my old friends moved on, and I'm out of touch with many of them, mostly because their ungodly liberal beliefs keep us apart; the truth of Jesus, and homey, does not play that anymore.

- 40 -
UNGODLY POLITICAL CLIMATE

I must talk about what is going on in America right now before I finish this book. It is not political, and it is not to hurt anyone; it is just what I feel the Lord has put on my heart to talk about.

I think it is sick that in New York, Democrats passed a law where you can kill (abort) babies now at birth. There is a video of the Democrats clapping after they passed the law, as if they won the Super Bowl. Keep your eyes on the hate spirit that has been coming alive, growing in America, after Obama was in office. Obama pushed his lies and hate on conservative Christians and white people, and mainstream leftist liberal news media is helping evil divide America by color, with hate. And of course, the pedophiles in Hollywood are joining the war on conservative pro-life Christians. Why? Mostly because we are pro-life, and we respect Israel and the God of Israel.

The liberal leftists have been infected with more hate than usual because the media and Hollywood said so. The world is under this witchcraft of hate too. And I am sure globalists and communists around the world are adding to this division of America.

Barack Obama is responsible for some of the hate as well. Obama was putting the Crusaders down for their past sins, putting down the Bible, slamming Christian and Jewish people, and saying things about the state of Israel that were not nice. I have never seen such hate until Obama and the media started spreading the hate.

Obama was going to do a speech at a Christian school, but unless they covered the cross in the background, he was not going to appear. Really? It is a scary day we live in today. If you do not believe me, do a web search; it is there on video.

Social media keeps deleting true stories and videos, hiding conservative Christian posts, while lifting the liberal leftist hate on conservatives, calling true facts conspiracy theories, like the 2020 election where we have eyewitnesses, videos, and whistleblowers, all saying voter fraud on a massive scale has taken place.

So sad, even Americans display disrespect for our flag, our national anthem, the police, and the military. What is next? Communism? That is the scary part. Ungodly people are taking control of our Washington, politics, the FBI, and the CIA. They are getting very bold in our face, and the media just covers it up. It is a sad day in America, and mainstream news media is leading the charge. Fake news and liberal Democrats and some Republicans are trying to blame everything bad on Trump. He is trying to help all Americans, and up to this point has done more for all Americans than the last three presidents, in my opinion.

It looks like most Americans now have turned away from God. That is a dangerous place to be.

It is sickening to watch news channels sympathizing with foreigners over the killing of Americans. Terrorists are killing people, chopping their heads off, and burning them alive on video for the world to see. China has waged war on the world by creating viruses, using their money to buy and sell hate, stealing US technology, and they paid Hunter Biden millions of dollars, trying to buy their way into Washington. Few news channels will report these things. Liberal media will report half-truths on conservatives on the right, and they have no problem calling conservatives racist or dirty names because they're different or have different political or different religious views.

I am seeing this ungodly hate growing. Evil is what it is. Most people who hate Jewish people and Christians do not really understand why they hate them. Liberal media gives them a reason to hate, and it is like witchcraft. It is not just the Democrats, but soon the Republicans, will join in with the globalists, and NATO's One World Order will be set up. Unless patriotic Americans fight this take over, we will become a Communist country. I am not saying fight with weapons. Being a Christian, we fight with prayer and the Word of God, in truth.

The Bible talks about how this evil is growing. It is satanic evil spirits that are taking over the minds of many people. Even after the truth comes out, few news channels will report that they had it wrong. They just let the hate grow rather than set the record straight.

I did not want to drag politics into this mix, but I think it is important to understand another way evil is creeping into our houses and our thoughts. This is really a warning of how evil finds its way into the hearts and minds of the people through the media.

Give your free time to God. It is important to remember a lifetime is short enough as it is. The heart of man is the same today as in the past; it is corrupted and cannot be fixed without Jesus. Time looks full, and the great harvest of souls is at hand, and the workers are few.

- 41 -
AMERICA MUST TURN TO JESUS

America must be united and get back to "In God We Trust" if we are to make it through the winds of change. This next world struggle will be the ugliest so far. The Bible says there will be a great falling away from truth just before the return of Jesus; it seems to be happening right now. This is another sign of the times, like in the days of Noah; people would be having fun, getting married, having parties, and celebrating, then sudden destruction.

Another passage in the Bible, in Daniel 12:4 (NIV), says we would see knowledge suddenly increase. I think that refers to the computer age. Right? There is more scripture, but there is not enough time to share them all. Search it out if you want to see for yourself. God is watching.

Hate is taking us back in time now, telling us we were a white racist nation. Yes, America was. I think there will always be racism, but it is not like it was. It is getting better. We, as a people, have come so far; now is not the time to turn back to hate.

There are lots of haters of all colors and political views. The truth is, the devil is out to get us, and he does not care what color you are. Evil will use anything and everything to get people to hate each other, even the truth. At some point, Americans should move forward, not resurrect our evil past.

It has taken four hundred years, but America has transformed into a great place. If you compare it to other countries, it is the best free nation in the world. If this is not true, why do so many people risk their lives trying to come here? Freedom in today's world is priceless. Every country in the world has a bloody history; this is our nature.

American people are under attack like never before: from within, our own people, and from other countries; their religions and cultures are hurting America, breaking us apart.

Evil has worked its way into the schools, into colleges, and even into Washington, mixing in, working side by side with Americans. Remember what happened at a Christmas party a couple years ago in San Bernardino, California? A terrorist Muslim wife and her husband murdered their coworkers and friends at a Christmas party. It is getting harder to trust people because of their religious beliefs. Some leaders teach these people to hate infidels, and some religions want to kill our way of life in America. China is clearly becoming another threat to the world.

Some politicians are getting so rich making big money to join the hate on conservatives, Christians, whites, and the people of Israel. The Bible says the evil will come like never before. Hate can be invisible like the wind, and it moves people. Satan wants to kill everything that God created and anyone who keeps His commandments and has faith in Jesus (Revelation 14:12 (NIV)).

God hates things, yes, but it is a godly hate, not evil hate like people have for the things God calls good.

Have you ever seen Christians or Jews make videos of chopping off heads or burning people alive? I do not think so, but the hate grows against them. I am not saying all Christians and Jews are perfect. I am saying, in Christian churches or Jewish synagogues, you do not see them making videos of murdering people, selling or preaching murderous hate.

After Hitler and his hate demons took power, they started burning history books, tearing down statues, trying to erase the past of the world's documents and monuments, like what we see happening in America right now. Socialism leads to communism; it always does. It starts with free stuff, promises, lies, and then they teach who to hate. It sounds and looks good but ends in death. God's Word will live on.

At some point, the hate war the left is starting and will reach a max out point in America; it will explode in blood. Hate and lies at any cost are the same thing the politicians and media did to the Native Americans to get their land. They got people to hate them, then took away their weapons and their ability to fight back to stay free.

Politicians are spending billions of dollars on hate words to attack people who speak the truth rather than spending money on fixing things for all Americans, no matter your color or religion, so all people can have a better life.

- 42 -
ISRAEL IS GOD'S TIME CLOCK

Adam and Eve's kids were born into the cursed world, and Cain committed the first recorded murder. There was a day where murder became like abortion; if you do not like it, kill it. We cannot let the system of death, which is the beast, rule our hearts and this land anymore. Can we even stop it? Yes, we can; with God, anything is possible. Jesus said we know not what to pray for. Hello.

So watch (see Revelation 3:3 (NIV)). If you do not watch, God will come on you like a thief in the night. I know I say things two or three times. In the Bible, God repeats His Words, I think, to burn it into your mind.

The Bible is clear: There will be three major world wars concerning Israel and God's people. During the last brutal, ugly war, God will cut it short to save people from complete destruction. A remnant of His church will be left to finish preaching the truth to the survivors. The real peacemaker, Jesus, will come to save what is left and stop the suffering. Thank God.

I believe America will play a big part in God's plan in the end with Israel.

I am glad our former president, Donald Trump, is a strong man. He is not perfect, but I do believe he loves America, babies, and Americans. I don't know what kind of relationship he has with God, but like all of us, we wrestle with things in our flesh and come to truth at some point. President Trump says he believes in Jesus, he is pro-life, and to me, this is better than saying he does not believe in God.

One drunken night, drunk on the Spirit of God, that is, the first group of Christians decided to never forget what Jesus did on the cross, so they started a new calendar. Most of the world uses that calendar today. It was that important for all the generations to come to never forget the miracles of God's power and His Son, Who came back from the dead. This memory can never be forgotten. Jesus is Lord over all heaven and earth, paying the sin debt in full.

It is not easy to understand why He had to pay with His blood or why God wanted our sin debt paid for by His Son. That is another long story you can read in God's Word. It is better if you read it there, rather than my watered-down version. Trust me, reading it firsthand from scripture is always better than having it relayed by a person. After you begin to understand His Word, then you can see how God's plan of salvation is perfect. Study His Word personally; it will be the best choice you could ever do for yourself, friends, and family.

Time as we see it today was set to start on that finished work of Christ on the cross. The world was turned upside down that day. The people of the day said Jesus must be in our history books for all time, from this day forward. The haters want to remove God from everything. The devil and evil spirits control their minds and souls.

It is all documented in time. People have been watching the Word of God unfold for many years; people like me and you know it to be true. Amen. It is all in the Bible. It has not changed much, maybe a couple words here and there, because of different translations, but it is all good. You cannot stop God's Word from getting out.

When you receive Jesus as Lord and get off dope, stop drinking, stop abusing others, and stop killing, which is a miracle. When one person gets saved, all the angels in heaven rejoice, clap, and say, "Holy, Holy, Holy is the Lamb of God Who takes away the sins of the world, the Lord Jesus."

After you look at about six thousand years of documenting Jewish history, compressed down to one book, the Bible, you can see Jehovah God bringing His plan to the world. The Jewish people had no idea, in the beginning to the end, their God was Jesus. He would bring the plan of salvation to the whole world, not just to the Jewish people.

Even now, have you ever been approached by a Jewish person without Jesus, for God's salvation plan? I never have.

Love God with all your heart, body, mind, and soul first; it will pay off. Another of God's promises. Get closer to God and have a better relationship with Him.

He is making His case inside your heart, body, mind, and soul, all at the same time. Do not be afraid now. Without putting your faith in Jesus, you can never satisfy God. We are all born sinners, separated spiritually from God, lost, and dying. As time goes on, we grow spiritually and find that narrow road that leads to life.

Every day, I try and stay close to the things of God, spiritually and in the flesh. I walk out each day, knowing I have not given up.

The heavenly Father leaves behind evidence and treasures to keep you interested in the supernatural hunt of eternal life. Jesus said I came to give, not take away.

The Bible helps us overcome sin and death, and live a better life while we are alive and help others find this truth. The road to destruction is wide, and the road to eternal life is narrow, and few will find it.

The Bible says every eye will see Jesus coming in the air with His saints (Revelation 1:7(NIV)).

Believe the impossible. It is hard to think how every eye could see Jesus coming in the air at the same time. The TV had to be invented first for that to happen. This is my opinion. I also think Satan, the great deceiver, will use the media to deceive the world too, so watch and be careful what you see and hear and believe in.

Timing is good to know about, such as the end-time's last big war. According to the Bible, this cannot start until after God's people, Israel, take back their land three times on recorded Jewish history; in 1945, World War II ended, and Jews were set free; in 1948, the nation of Israel was formed by the Jewish people; and in 1967, the famous Six-Day War, recorded by many, was a supernatural war.

If you hear the testimonies from the enemies of the Jewish people about the Six-Day War, then you would know that God's hand was in that war. The enemies fighting the Jewish people said there was a great delusion in their eyes of a massive Israeli army coming at them. So they ran for their lives. The truth is, Israel had a very small force up against a much larger army, but on God's time and God's power, the Jewish people took back the land, Israel, and they have to rebuild their temple for the last time before Jesus returns. From what I hear, they are building the last temple right now.

If you look at ancient writings, you will see how the Jewish people have been fighting, losing, and winning wars for the land and to just exist. Even right into modern times, Israel has been under attack over the land. But the truth is, it is not the land they really all want. It is the evil hatred the world has for the Jewish people and their God, Jesus.

Fake news media is buying into the hate by saying Israel took the land from the Palestinians; not true. Nowhere in the writings, from long ago, does God say He gave the Palestinians this land. Another reason the world hates God's Word is because the Jewish people are the chosen ones in the Old Testament. Jesus came to open His salvation plan to all people. So if the people of the world were smart, they would stop hating and come to the God of Israel, Jesus, and get saved by His love, putting their faith in Christ's shed blood at the cross.

Salvation does not come by the lies and evil-spirited hate of the gods of this world. The Bible says most of them will not come to Jesus; so sad for them.

Most of you only hear what the fake news tells you about the struggles of the Palestinians, so some of you sympathize with the half-lies and begin to hate Jewish people. Some of you have been misled, so be careful not to fall for evil-spirited hate against people you do not know much about.

I say, yes, we should hand this land back to the Indians so they can run it the way they want to. I realize this will never happen, and the haters in the world will do what they want, like the Bible says they would. If you want to know where the world is in time, watch the people of Israel, God's time clock in history. In the past, the Bible showed us where we are as a people in the world, and it's doing so now too. You can see how things are lined up perfectly, and time is full. The stage is set up for God's last few prophecies to finish unfolding. The Lord will destroy evil. The cameras are rolling as we speak, to catch this next supernatural event so all can see like Christ on the cross, hung up high, for all to see how evil it is, so keep watching.

The big last war will start with Israel defending their land, or Israel will take the first big strike to set it off.

"Remember, therefore, what you have received and heard; hold it fast, and repent. Keep it, and repent. If you will not wake up, I will come like a thief, and you will not know at what hour I will come against you" (Revelation 3:3 (NIV)).

I personally think Israel will say we've had enough of this hate and death. Israel will cast the biggest stone ever, and the world will revolt against them, like the scripture says. Then the God of Israel will rise to beat down the evil rulers and haters against God's church. They have hated His people for so long, past, present, and into the future. God will cast the haters and the people who reject Christ Jesus into the lake of fire, and then God's kingdom will be set up on earth, and there will be everlasting peace.

I was a clown; now, I'm a man of God.

"Clown"

"Soaring with Eagles"

Soaring with the eagles

- 43 -
DON'T SUPPORT THE BEAST WITH YOUR VOTE

The Bible in its totality is one of the greatest building blocks of life, given by God to His people and the world. The Father brings His plan of salvation to humanity's table.

If you try talking about Jesus to friends or to family members, most of them will say it is not the right time; it never seems to be the right time. Jesus says people of God must leave his hometown, go out, and preach to people they do not know. Or write a book, because most family and friends do not believe God would pick you or me to be His disciple, teacher, preacher, or peacemaker.

In today's world, children of God should stick out like a bump on a log. But most Christians blend into this world well because they have been taught not to offend anyone, to be silent, sometimes even in their own homes. Most Christians will be okay with not talking about Jesus, in fear they will be rejected by people. No, not you, other people, of course. You are not afraid to hear about God or to be bold in Jesus and preach it. Are you?

Jehovah God is the God of life.

Freedom, prosperity, and justice for all. Over four hundred years ago, America started out with those principles in mind: God and country. The land grabbed from the Native Americans was wrong. Slavery was wrong. Murder has always been wrong, and the color of your skin has nothing to do with the power struggle people have. Black people kill black people. White people kill white people. I believe if a person is evil enough to kill another person, it probably does not really matter what color they are. Yes, some white people do not like black people, and some black people do not like white people. If everybody received Jesus as Lord, murder would end. If you are defending your family member or your own life from an evil killer, it is possible that death can occur, but remember self-defense is different from murder. Can we all agree on that? Lots of horrible things that went on in history were wrong.

The problem most people are having is spiritual, not the color of our skin or what part of the world we came from or how much money we have. Evil wants war. Racism can be used as a tool to get people to hate and fight. Yes, racism is alive and always will be, but the deeper problem is supernatural, not in the flesh. "For we wrestle not against flesh and blood, but against principalities, against powers, against the rulers of the darkness of this world" (Ephesians 6:12 (NIV)).

We must stay united as a nation under God, or we'll lose this baby fast.

I am not writing this book to condemn any one group or party of people. My testimony may sound political at times, but it is not meant to be. Another sad part to this truth is America, the world, has become political about everything, so it is hard not to talk about the environment we find ourselves in now. This book is not for votes for office. I am reflecting on what I see in today's system of the beast. Evil is floating into the political realm, big and fast. We can use God's Word to help expose where the evil is. Our government has crossed over completely into the dark side of evil. Long ago, politicians, the FBI, the CIA, news media, and Hollywood actors began coordinating together to generate a narrative, working behind the scenes in Washington on TV, the radio, and the internet to keep power over the people. This should scare everyone, no matter who you vote for or what party you belong to, even if you do not believe in God. This truth breaks political lines on both sides. We should worry about that. But fewer and fewer Americans are worried, so it seems. Most people cannot see this beast. The Antichrist is building his army in the world and is taking power in America's political system.

The Pilgrims moved away from the dictators, kings, and queens of the past ages to be free from this tyranny of evil, ungodly rulers. After four hundred years, though, it has crept back into our lives again. Isn't it funny how only true believers in Jesus can see this evil creeping into our everyday lives? Liberal media and Hollywood are on board with this darkness and lies. Why is this? Good question, because the ungodly world is eating out of the hands of the beast, which is the spirit of the Antichrist. The Antichrist knows how to get you to take his mark without a fight. Food, lies, free stuff, money, and now, Covid-19 seem to be ways to control the world.

Someday soon, this book you are reading, along with other Christian books and the Bible, will be against the law, because it exposes the evil in the media, Hollywood, politics, and the ungodly world, lost without Jesus.

You need to know the God of Israel, Father of Abraham, Isaac, and Jacob. Why, Buster, why? Because back a couple thousand years ago, people had different gods. Even today, there are different gods. People make up names of gods or are adopted into families with other gods of this world.

If I was talking to you at the marketplace one rainy day, getting to know you, I might ask, "Who is your god? Does he have a name? Can he turn water into wine or part the Red Sea? Did he come back from the dead?"

No. There are lots of people and lots of gods in this world, and they all have a story to tell. Years ago, talking to people about gods, the Jews would say their God is the God of Abraham, Isaac, and Jacob, the God of Israel. That is my God. He never changes who He is. He only revealed to us who He is in Jesus.

Islamic people also believe they descended from Abraham. But the promises of the Messiah, the Savior Jesus, did not come down the blood line of any other tribe or people other than the Jewish people. Why? Because the Lord said so. The Old Testament said the Messiah would come from the blood line of King David, down to Mary and Joseph. Same blood line as King David. Bible study makes this clear and easy to understand. This is important to know because if you get adopted into the family of this God, you should know who your family is and their history so you can be clear and grounded in the one God. Jesus is the Lord, not the Islamic god Allah, or Buddha, or any other god (certainly not Satan, the god of this world).

- 44 -
THE JEWS, MUSLIMS, AND CHRISTIANS WILL UNITE

I am building up to the good stuff.

I really feel I must drill this one point into your minds and spirit. Remember, God is the God of Israel. The Bible has us watching His plan unfold, for the last few promises to come to pass. Stay clear of people who hate Jews and Christians; your life will improve, I promise.

We wrestle not against flesh and blood but principalities, powers, and evil rulers in high dark places. Read Ephesians 6:12 (NIV). I did not understand this all at first, but after Bible study, it began to make sense. God showed me. He proved to me He is the true God, Creator of life in His Word, the Bible, and all things are possible with Him.

Discover God in the Old Testament, and watch how He comes alive for all to see, hung high on the tree in the New Testament.

The Christian church, the Jews, Muslims, and other tribes around the world are spiritual brothers. And I do believe at some point, Jews and Muslims will unite together with Christians and receive Jesus as Lord.

People today say there are many gods and many ways to heaven; this is not true. There is only one true God, one plan, and one way in.

The Bible has a beginning theme, and the prophecies conclude to an end; it has been proven to be true throughout time.

I wanted this book to be easy to read so anyone could understand it. Big words do not help people understand how simple saying yes to Jesus is.

The Lord knows how many hairs are on your head. That is how in detail He is for each one of us and how much love He has. There is something in you that you might not know about. Yes, in you right now, waiting for you to discover it by faith. The Bible says something great is in you, hiding so the thief cannot steal it from you. It is your faith, one of the tools you need to please God.

Everything does happen for a reason. What the Lord gives us is freely given. The blood of Christ does not wash off with soap and water, thank God.

So move closer to the good things God has for us. Let us rest in knowing what you need is inside you, hidden from thieves. Get past thinking God's not happy with you. Find your miracle today. Cross the line of doubt. Jesus uses love to heal us. It grows inside us and gives life eternal forever. Jesus did draw a line in the sand, and I hope you are on His side of that line.

Reading the Bible is the best way to discover Who God is and how He speaks to us.

Let God ride into your life; let the winds move your soul and be washed by the blood of Christ Jesus.

Romans 8:28 (NIV) says all things work for the good of those who are called according to His purpose and that love Him.

- 45 -
READ GOD'S WORD

Covid-19 hit the world more than a year ago, under the forty-fifth president of the United States. I am at home under quarantine finishing this book. I must finish this book now and get it to the publisher because it is anyone's guess if it will make it out to the public before Jesus returns. I am praying it will.

God is shaking the earth and humankind, so be still and watch the Lord work as the death angel passes over our homes and down our streets. Did God make this virus? No, but He did allow it. I think technology is doing most of the damage to people. 5G high frequency internet waves are making people sick. It seems the beast is at work with the Antichrist in the world, and this virus is being used to make their move on humankind, for the mark of the beast, for power, and to decrease the population in the world.

God's people will fight with the Word of the Lord as their swords and stand in their way; with the Lord's help, anything is possible. Fear not, turn from your sins, repent, and follow Jesus. In the morning, His mercies are new. "Go, my people, enter your rooms and shut the doors behind you, hide yourselves for a little while until His wrath has passed by." (Isaiah 26:20 (NIV)).

First Thessalonians 5:1-9 (NIV) says, "Now, brothers and sisters, about times and dates we do not need to write to you, for you know very well the day of the Lord will come like a thief in the night. While people are saying peace and safety, destruction will come on them suddenly, as labor pains on a pregnant woman, and they will not escape. But you, brothers and sisters, are not in darkness so that this day should surprise you like a thief. You are children of the light and children of the day. We do not belong to the night or to the darkness. So then, let us not be like others, who are asleep, but let us be awake and sober. For those who sleep, sleep at night, and those who get drunk, get drunk at night. But since we belong to the day, let us be sober, putting on faith and love as breast plate, and the hope of salvation as a helmet. For God did not appoint us to suffer wrath but to receive to salvation through our Lord Jesus Christ. He died for us so that, whether we are awake or asleep, we may live together with him."

Psalm 44:7 (NIV) says, "But you give us victory over our enemies, you put our adversaries to shame."

Matthew 7:7 (NIV) says, "Ask, and it shall be given to you; seek, and you shall find; knock, and the door will be opened unto you."

John 10:10 (NIV) says, "The thief comes only to steal and kill, and to destroy; I have come that they may have life, and they may have it to the full."

1 Peter 4:10 (NIV) says, "Each of you should use whatever gift you have received to serve others, as faithful stewards of God's grace in its various forms."

Read the whole chapter of Matthew 24. It says a lot about the end days and signs before Jesus comes, and things to watch for.

- 46 -
A WORLD WITHOUT END

See Isaiah 45:17 (NIV), which says, "But Israel shall be saved in the Lord with an everlasting salvation: you will never be put to shame or disgraced, to ages everlasting." I am writing to you; trust me, my words are easier to listen to and are not very scary. There are times when God speaks to His people; it could be scary and create fear. To understand what I just said, you have to read Exodus 19:16 (NIV). In short, the Lord was speaking with great sounds of thunder and lightning, and the people said to Moses, "Speak to us yourself and we will listen. But do not have God speak to us or we will die." Also read Exodus 20:18-19 (NIV).

Psalm 27:1-2 (NIV) says, "The Lord is my light and my salvation; whom shall I fear? The Lord is the stronghold of my life of whom shall I be afraid? When evil men advance against me to devour my flesh, when my enemies and my foe attack me, they will stumble and fall."

Luke 24:44-49 (NIV) says, "He said to them, This is what I told you while I was still with you: everything must be fulfilled that was written about Me in the Law of Moses and the prophets and the Psalms. Then He opened their minds so they could understand the scriptures. He told them this is what is written that Christ will suffer and rise from the dead on the third day. And repentance and forgiveness of sins will be preached in His name to all nations, beginning at Jerusalem. You are witnesses of these things. I am going to send you what my Father has promised; but stay in the city until you have been clothed with power from on high."

I believe Jesus was saying that they would be filled with the fire of the Holy Spirit on the day of Pentecost. Read Acts 2.

After tasting the things of God, you would never purposely walk away from the truth. That is why you will not lose your salvation. The Word of God says after being saved by Jesus, covered in His blood, nothing can snatch you from His hands. Nothing, not even your sins, because you will learn to hate sin, like God does. Therefore, your salvation is secure in Him, so rest in knowing that. To me, knowing that His strong hand is securing your salvation is the perfect salvation plan. God's love for one person is as strong as for all nations, and He is perfect in His judgments and all His ways.

God of creation, the God of Israel, Father of Abraham, Isaac, and Jacob says before His plan is over, every knee will bow, and every tongue will confess Jesus is Lord.

May your hunt for the truth be filled with wisdom, knowledge, faith, grace, mercy, understanding, and love. Walk in the love of Jesus every moment. Do not be afraid to ask for your miracles. Follow His voice of reason. May the Lord lead every person who is reading this to their salvation plan. Give them the power to read and understand Your Word, and may You bless and protect the readers and their families.

Thank you for reading my book; in Jesus's name, I pray. Amen.

CONCLUSION

I want to thank Judy, my wife, for helping me with this book and all ten of our kids and grandkids for being good, respectful, hard-working, and loving. Thank you, Judy, for believing in me from day one and giving me everything I've ever asked of you (and more). She never complains and is always giving to our kids, never thinking of herself first. Thank you, Lord, for bringing Judy and me back together. She is my perfect blue-eyed momma. We are equally yoked. I needed her love so much in my life. She is my best friend, my coworker, and the love of my life. Lord, keep giving me the love I need to respect, cherish, and take care of her, our children, and grandchildren.

Most of all, thank You, Jesus for being my King, my Rock, and the Ark of my salvation, and for saving me from the darkness and teaching me how to love people better. You are my God of Israel. Amen.

Lord Jesus, I wrote my testimony and put it in a book, like you asked. Now do Your part, save souls, and if it be Your will, let it be a best-seller all around the world. Take it to the ends of the earth, and show the people how awesome You are. Amen.

Printed in the United States
by Baker & Taylor Publisher Services